WEST SUSSEX
UNDER ATTACK

WEST SUSSEX
UNDER ATTACK

ANTI-INVASION SITES
1500-1990

CHRIS BUTLER

The History Press

This book is dedicated to my son Elijah

First published in 2008
Reprinted 2010

The History Press
The Mill, Brimscombe Port,
Stroud, Gloucestershire, GL5 2QG
www.thehistorypress.co.uk

British Library Cataloguing in Publication Data.
A catalogue record for this book is available from the British Library.

ISBN 978 0 7524 4171 9

Typesetting and origination by The History Press
Printed and bound in Great Britain

CONTENTS

ILLUSTRATIONS

TEXT FIGURES

COLOUR PLATES

ACKNOWLEDGEMENTS

Numerous people have helped me with my survey and during the production of this book. I would especially like to thank, Luke Barber, Ian Budd, Dave Cudmore, Trevor Davies, David Dunstall, Michael Fairbrother, Martin Hayes, Peter Hibbs, Richard Hurley, Jeremy Knight, Michael Leppard, Ron Martin, John Mills, Geoff Muir, John Salt, Paul Sims, Liza Stewart and Richard Wells. Sue Rowland prepared the maps used in this book. I would especially like to thank Rachel for her help and support.

PREFACE

The objective of this book is to provide a guide to the surviving post-medieval defence sites in West Sussex, following on from my earlier book on East Sussex. This period covers all types of site from the Tudor batteries through to sites of the Cold War era. Although focusing on anti-invasion sites, a whole range of defence sites are considered, including barracks, training centres and civil defence sites such as air-raid shelters. This book is the result of a long-standing interest of mine in aspects of warfare and has enabled me to combine this with my archaeological knowledge to draw on the evidence, both desk-based and field-based, in an attempt to understand the defensive landscapes of West Sussex. West Sussex is very different from East Sussex, both in its landscape and in the number of sites that survive. West Sussex has seen more development, especially on the coastal plain, which has removed many of the sites thus resulting in a smaller number surviving to be recorded today. Furthermore, inland in East Sussex there are surviving examples of Nodal Points, which are almost completely absent in West Sussex. One category of site that West Sussex does have more of is airfields; these are numerous and mostly located on the coastal plain and have been grouped together in their own chapter in this book.

As well as my own research accumulated over many years, I have used the *Defence of Britain* database as a starting point in gathering information. This has to be used with care, however, due to the incorrect data held within some of the records. Common problems include incorrect grid references and multiple records for the same site, each with slightly differing information recorded by different individuals. Local museums and historical societies have also been contacted and much useful information has been provided by these sources. The West Sussex Library Service at Worthing Library has provided access to its extensive reference collection, as well as many photographs from the Second World War. After this desk-top research, I have visited each site to record the in situ remains first hand, often following this up with further site visits to answer questions that arise when considering the data I have collected. I have also talked to local landowners, other archaeologists and historians, together with people who lived in the area during the Second World War, to collect oral evidence. This has frequently meant that additional previously unrecorded sites (both extant and removed) have been rediscovered. As well as producing this book, all of the accumulated data has been incorporated into a database, which will be deposited with the county and National Monuments Record.

Although this book covers the whole period from 1500 through to the Cold War, there is a strong focus on sites of the Second World War, as these are the main types of site that survive today. It has also become very apparent to me whilst conducting this survey that many of the surviving sites are under great threat, and are not always appreciated as being of historical importance. On occasion I have gone to visit a previously recorded site only to find it is no longer there, and some existing sites are under a variety of threats today. A recent example of this was seen last year at Shoreham Airfield, when a tracked excavator cleaning out the drainage ditch along the east side of the airfield drove across the roof of the partly sunken air-raid shelter causing damage to the roof and weakening the whole structure.

One thing that has become very obvious as I have researched these books for East and West Sussex is that as I have scratched the surface of each site, new things have emerged, and there is still much more out there to be discovered and recorded. Therefore, this book should be considered little more than a current statement of our knowledge,and will be the first stage of a larger survey, which will involve more detailed desk-top research to fill the missing gaps. I know there will have been some sites that I have missed and I would be pleased to receive any information on these.

One of the fascinating aspects of the survey for me has been the interest that many landowners and others have in what these bits of concrete are that they have on their land, and the pride that many of them have in looking after the sites. It has also been inspiring to visit sites and see that an owner is making good and sensible use of a pillbox or other feature in their garden or on their land, as this will ultimately help to preserve it for the future. Frequently landowners have been able to provide me with additional information about their sites and, without exception, have been pleased to let me visit sites on their land and record them.

Please note: The inclusion of a site in this book does not imply that you can visit it. Whilst many sites are on public access land or alongside public rights of way, you should always obtain permission before visiting a site on private land.

1

INTRODUCTION

It is not my intention to provide a historical account of the period, as there are many other sources for this information and the bibliography in this book should be consulted for more general background reading on this subject. However, to put the sites into their historical context, this chapter includes a brief description of each major period relevant to the book and discusses the different types of site, explaining their construction and function. The chapter concludes with an outline of how the book is organised and suggestions as to how to use it to see the surviving sites.

THE HISTORICAL CONTEXT

The Tudor period saw many changes in warfare, with artillery beginning to dominate combat both on land and at sea. The medieval castle had been in decline for some time; during the Tudor period it was replaced by artillery forts and batteries built to protect ports and at possible landing places along the south coast. Although there were no artillery forts in West Sussex, a number of earthen batteries were constructed to defend potential landing sites. These batteries generally comprised a rampart of earth thrown up from a ditch, sometimes with a timber palisade added to the top of the rampart. Cannons were then positioned on a platform behind the rampart, the number varying from place to place.

The entire Sussex coast was particularly vulnerable to cross-Channel raids; Brighton was attacked in 1514, while in July 1545 a French fleet made an attack on the south coast after an engagement at Portsmouth in which the *Mary Rose* was sunk. On the 21 July 1545 a French fleet was off Brighton, and on the 22 July a French force landed at Seaford in East Sussex. The wars with France ended when Calais was ceded to the French and during the reign of Elizabeth I wars with Spain led to a shift in focus to the south-west of England. A system of fire beacons was used to provide warning of an attack and the coastal batteries in West Sussex were manned during 1588 when the Spanish Armada threatened the coast.

After this coastal defences went into a period of decline and abandonment. The English Civil War had more of an impact on West Sussex than it had on East Sussex, with major sieges at Chichester (Site 11) and Arundel Castle (Site 14), and a number of small battles and skirmishes, including those at Bramber (Site 20) and Haywards Heath (Site 24).

There was very little military activity in West Sussex during the eighteenth century until the last decade, when events on the continent sparked a major programme of rebuilding. However, a new battery had been built at Littlehampton in 1760, replacing an earlier redundant battery nearby, to protect the mouth of the River Arun.

The threat from revolutionary France and then from Napoleon saw the largest concentration of military activity in Sussex up to that point, as defences were put into place, and regular troops and militia were installed in garrisons across the county to face the expected invasion. A line of 73 Martello towers constructed along the Kent and East Sussex coasts stopped at Seaford and did not continue into West Sussex, although new batteries were built at Selsey and Bognor, and signal stations were constructed at intervals along the coast.

Inland and along the coast, dozens of barracks were built to take the *c.*20,000 regular and militia soldiers that flooded into Sussex. These varied from small temporary camps on the South Downs through to large permanent barracks holding hundreds of soldiers such as those at Chichester (Site 11) and Horsham (Site 27). The majority of these barracks were wooden buildings with thatched or tiled roofs, and most were sold off and dismantled at the end of the Napoleonic Wars.

After the Napoleonic Wars there was another period of decay, with many of the forts and batteries being lost to coastal erosion or neglect. However, in the later part of the nineteenth century a new French invasion scare initiated yet another phase of defence works, with new forts being constructed at Littlehampton (*1*) and Shoreham. Again the expected threat did not materialise and by the end of the nineteenth century the fortifications along the West Sussex coast had all been abandoned.

The First World War had little initial impact on West Sussex, but later there was a huge influx of soldiers into the county, with training camps set up on the Downs and inland, and large areas of the countryside were used for training. Most of these camps have disappeared from the landscape, and subsequent agricultural activities have removed any evidence for them.

A new form of defence site made its appearance in the First World War; this was the airfield, associated either with aircraft or airships. A number of examples were located in West Sussex, including an airship outstation at Slindon (Site 13) and airfields at Rustington (Site 6), Goring (Site 7), Tangmere (Site 33), Ford (Site 36) and Shoreham (Site 37). A number of these were fairly substantial establishments, with hangars, maintenance and domestic buildings, some of which survived at the sites for many years after the war, whilst others were quickly removed. At

1 Littlehampton Fort from the air – showing the Carnot wall with open bastions at its corners, and the defensible barracks at the rear of the fort. Outside the rear of the fort there is an additional barracks hut

Selsey a sound mirror was built to detect aircraft and airships crossing the English Channel (Site 1).

The Second World War brought about the most extensive period of anti-invasion construction work ever seen and there were a number of significant differences from previous defence construction schemes. The first was the move away from just coastal defence sites to a network of defence lines along rivers and other obstacles, as well as the normal coastal defences. Secondly, in response to the changes that had taken place in warfare over the preceding decades, much greater emphasis was put on anti-aircraft defences. Finally, as the Luftwaffe could now bring the war directly to British towns there was a huge effort geared towards civil defence. The vast number of sites built during the war provides us with the best surviving evidence for anti-invasion sites, but it is a diminishing resource.

Along the beaches of West Sussex, barbed wire, mines, anti-tank scaffolding and cubes were laid (*2*), whilst pillboxes were sited at regular intervals. Emergency coastal batteries, utilising ex-naval guns from storage, were quickly set up to cover the most vulnerable landing places (*3*), whilst schemes for setting the sea alight with burning fuel were put in place at some locations. Inland, roadblocks and other obstructions were established at important points, and fields were blocked with poles, cables and trenches to stop aircraft and gliders landing. Stop lines were set up along rivers across the county to block the routes the Germans would be expected to take towards London and the west. The most important Stop Line in West Sussex was the Guildford to Uckfield Corps Stop Line, which ran from Guildford in Surrey, across West Sussex, and on to Uckfield in East Sussex. This Stop Line was not a continuous defensive line, but instead comprised pillboxes

2 Beach scaffolding on the open ground to the rear of the beach between Worthing and Lancing. *West Sussex County Council Library Service: PP/WSL/WGP00026.* www.westsussexpast.org.uk/pictures

3 The Worthing Emergency Coastal Battery on the promenade at the junction of West Parade and Grand Avenue. This photograph shows the rear of the two gun positions, which are disguised as bungalows. *West Sussex County Council Library Service: PP/WSL/WGP00040.* www.westsussexpast.org.uk/pictures

covering the road and railway crossings over the Rivers Ouse and Arun. Similar defences were constructed along the River Adur and River Arun to delay and prevent any invading forces moving easily westwards.

Towns and villages on important road and railway routes were designated as Nodal Points and put into a state of defence. Many were encircled with anti-tank

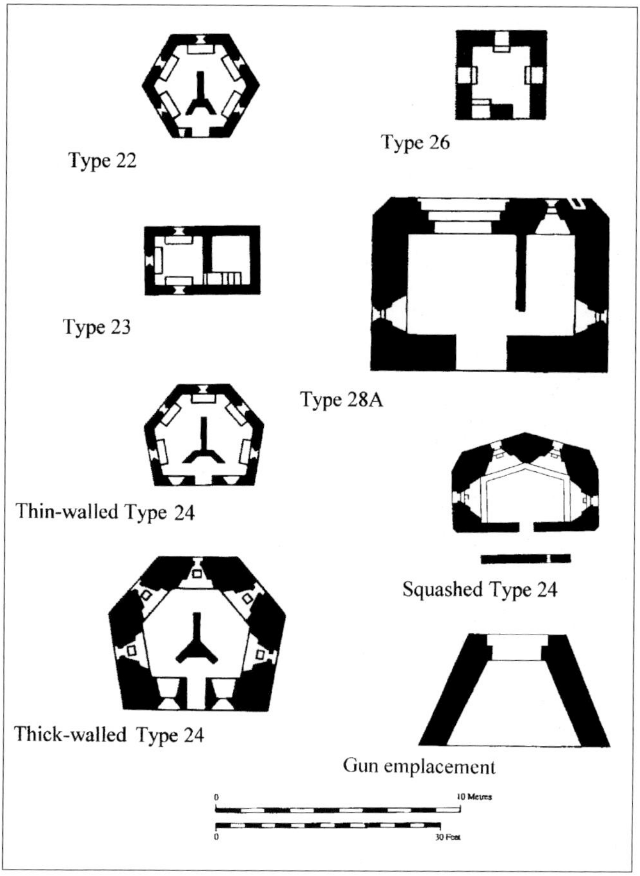

4 West Sussex Pillbox types: The Type 24 and Type 28 pillboxes were the most common types, especially along the Corps Stop Line. The Type 26 was frequently found on the coast, whilst the Type 23 only occurs on airfields. The Gun emplacement was a unique West Sussex variety, being found only along the rivers Adur and Arun. *Gun emplacement plan adapted from Ron Martin original drawing*

cubes supported by roadblocks, pillboxes, minefields and *flame fougasse* sites; they were expected to hold out against attack for a number of days in the event of an invasion.

There were a number of different standard types of pillbox used, although not all of them were found in West Sussex. There were also many different variants constructed to suit local requirements or dependent upon the materials and resources available at the time. The most common varieties of pillbox used in West Sussex are shown in figure 4, together with the unusual gun emplacements, which are unique to the Stop Lines along the rivers Arun and Adur. These open-backed artillery gun emplacements were probably intended to take either the 75mm M1917 guns that had been supplied by the Americans, or QF 13pdr or 18pdrs. Other forms of defences that survive today include the different types of anti-tank obstacles. Anti-tank cubes, coffins, pimples (dragons' teeth), cylinders and buoys were all used to form obstacles or roadblocks (5). The first three types were fixed defences, constructed in situ and often with a root extending below ground, coffins being found at roadblocks and bridges. Cylinders and anti-tank buoys were designed so that they could be moved from the roadside to form

5 A roadblock near Goring during the Second World War. This photograph shows all of the elements that made up a typical roadblock. Concrete cubes block the gap between the edge of the roadblock and adjacent hedge and ditch. In the road can be seen the sockets for the hairpin rails, whilst the rails themselves lie at the side of the road, along with a number of anti-tank buoys. *West Sussex County Council Library Service: PP/WSL/WGP00042*. www.westsussexpast.org.uk/pictures

roadblocks and frequently had metal poles in their tops for wire entanglements. They were often associated with curved rail (hairpin) roadblocks, the filled-in sockets for which can sometimes still be found in the road surface. Traces of anti-tank ditch rarely survive, as these were quickly filled in after the war. Anti-tank scaffolding on beaches was also quickly removed at the end of the war, but sometimes it was simply cut off at ground level so the bottoms of the scaffolding poles occasionally survive. Good descriptions of all of these types of defences are given in Lowry (1996).

There were a number of airfields located in West Sussex, especially in the Chichester area, at the start of the Second World War and these played a major part during the Battle of Britain, and then in taking the war to the enemy during the following years. Some civilian airfields were taken over and utilised for training and other operations. Later in the war a number of Advanced Landing Grounds (ALGs) were built to take the huge numbers of aircraft being massed for the D-Day landings, but these were short-lived and quickly reverted back to agriculture before the war ended.

West Sussex also had a number of important radar sites that formed part of the early warning Chain Home network across the south-east. These continued in use into the early Cold War period, but are all now dismantled and abandoned. A network of Observer Corps posts was set up across the county, reporting in to the

Sector HQ at Horsham. Despite being manned for most of the war, they tended to be of temporary construction and rarely survive, though they frequently used already existing suitable buildings which may still survive. Most anti-aircraft gun positions were also very temporary and only those for 3.7in HAA guns were more solidly built.

Civil defence sites were constructed in large numbers. Public air-raid shelters, generally either brick-built surface shelters with a concrete roof or below-ground shelters, were built in town centres, whilst Anderson shelters were provided to those who wanted them. Many buildings with cellars or basements were also used as air-raid shelters. ARP warden's posts often utilised existing buildings, but there were also many purpose-built structures as well. Other civil defence preparations included the setting up of first aid posts, fire-watchers posts and emergency water tanks for fire fighting purposes.

Large areas of West Sussex were utilised for training during the Second World War, with most of the South Downs becoming a restricted area. Numerous firing ranges were constructed in dry valleys for all sorts of weapons from rifles to tanks and artillery. To provide easy access to these training areas a series of concrete 'tank roads' were constructed onto the Downs, many of which survive today as farm tracks. Military camps sprang up across the county and often the buildings remained in use into the post-war period, although most of these sites have now been developed as housing or industrial units.

There are many other types of Second World War defence site that survive, one being the decoy sites, designed to provide decoys for towns, ports and airfields in the hope that German bombers would attack them instead of the real target. Furthermore, around Chichester Harbour (Site 11) and at other coastal locations, local shipbuilders were involved in the construction and repair of small boats and landing craft, especially during the build-up to D-Day.

Once the war was over, the defences were frequently cleared away very quickly. Seaside towns such as Worthing, with an eye on the summer tourist trade, brought in contractors to demolish pillboxes and remove the seafront anti-tank obstacles (*6*), although in inland areas it would take many years for local authorities to arrange clearance or compensation. Correspondence dating to 1947-1950 between landowners and Cuckfield Rural District Council discussing the categorisation of various defence installations still in place makes interesting reading, especially as some of the defences mentioned were subsequently never removed and survive to this day.

During the Cold War the emphasis moved away coastal and fixed lines of defence to the threat from the air and especially the threat from nuclear weapons. The front line, in terms of any ground war, had moved to Germany, and apart from a handful of military garrisons and Territorial Army Drill Halls there was little visible sign of defence sites in the county.

However, the air and nuclear threat was taken seriously, and a network of ROC underground monitoring posts was established across the county, still reporting to

6 Clearing away the defences at Worthing after the War: Taylor Woodrow were contracted to remove the anti-tank cubes around Worthing. This is one of a number of photographs that show this work being carried out. *West Sussex County Council Library Service: PP/WSL/WGP00041.* www.westsussexpast.org.uk/pictures

No. 2 Sector HQ at Horsham (Site 27). Although these were all decommissioned in the early 1990s many of the monitoring posts are still extant, although the Horsham HQ building has now been demolished.

Civil defence planning also changed to meet the new threats of the Cold War. Air-raid shelters for the general population were no longer seen as a realistic proposition, although underground bunkers for regional and sub-regional seats of government were established across the country. Instead the emphasis was put on providing resources for the surviving population after a nuclear strike. To this end numerous 'Buffer Depots' were established to hold supplies of food and other essentials.

From the end of the Cold War up to the present day, the story is one of abandonment and decline, with few active military installations now used in West Sussex. Redevelopment for housing and industrial units is seeing a dramatic decline in surviving Post-War military sites.

HOW TO USE THIS BOOK

There are three chapters in the book organised to take you first of all along the West Sussex coast from west (Selsey) to east (Hove). The second chapter looks at all of the inland sites including the larger towns of the county such as Chichester, Arundel, Horsham and East Grinstead, whilst also looking at some of the defence

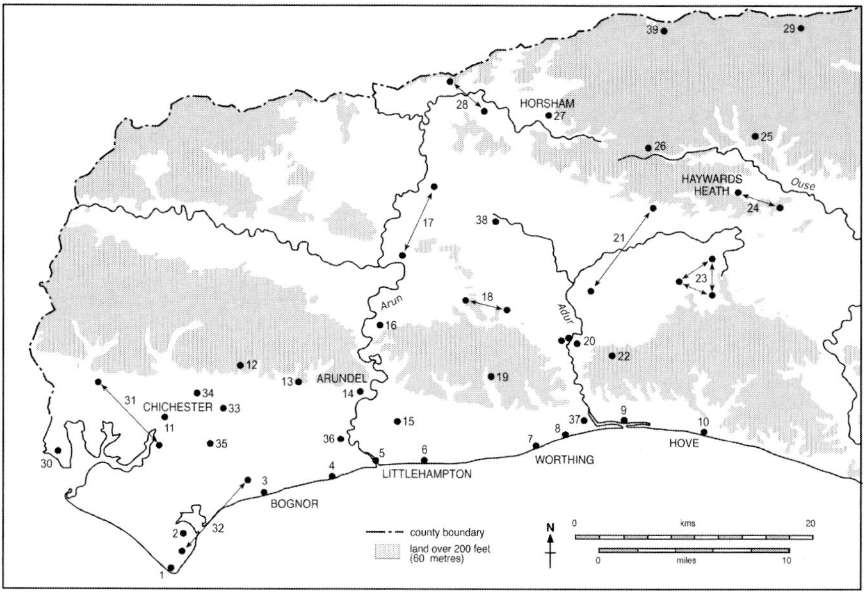

7 Map of West Sussex showing all of the sites covered in this book

lines including the Guildford to Uckfield Corps Stop Line. The final chapter looks at all of the airfields in West Sussex, including the ALGs. Many of the site locations are multi-period, so they cover all of the defence installations at the site from the Tudor period through to the Cold War. Each site entry starts with a brief historical outline to put the site into its context, explaining what was located there and why. The next section explains what is still there to be seen today and the final section gives directions on how to find the individual sites. Finally where there are specific references for sites they are given within that entry. The bibliography at the end of the book provides more general reading.

You will find an Ordnance Survey 1:25000 map is essential and to help find surviving sites (7), a grid reference is given for each one – eight-figure grid references have normally been recorded using a hand-held GPS, whilst six-figure grid references are estimated, perhaps where access was not possible. You should note that many sites are located alongside fast roads and in other dangerous locations, so please exercise care when looking for sites. The inclusion of any site in this book does not imply that you can visit it. Whilst many are on public access land or alongside public rights of way, all sites are owned by someone so if in doubt you should not visit a site without specifically obtaining permission to do so.

2

COASTAL SITES

The coastal region of West Sussex has not had the same intensive fortification that was seen in East Sussex throughout the whole of the period covered. In fact, apart from a few batteries and the two nineteenth-century forts at Littlehampton and Shoreham, the West Sussex coastline was only really fortified during the Second World War. However, the coastal towns in West Sussex frequently include other types of sites not directly related to defending the coastline and these are also covered in this chapter, along with a number of off-shore sites.

The sites covered in this chapter start at Selsey, at the west end of the county, and progress eastwards along the coast to finish at Hove (*8*). Brighton is included in the East Sussex book. Although Thorney Island on the Hampshire border is a coastal site, its main facility was an airfield so it is covered in Chapter 4 (Site 30).

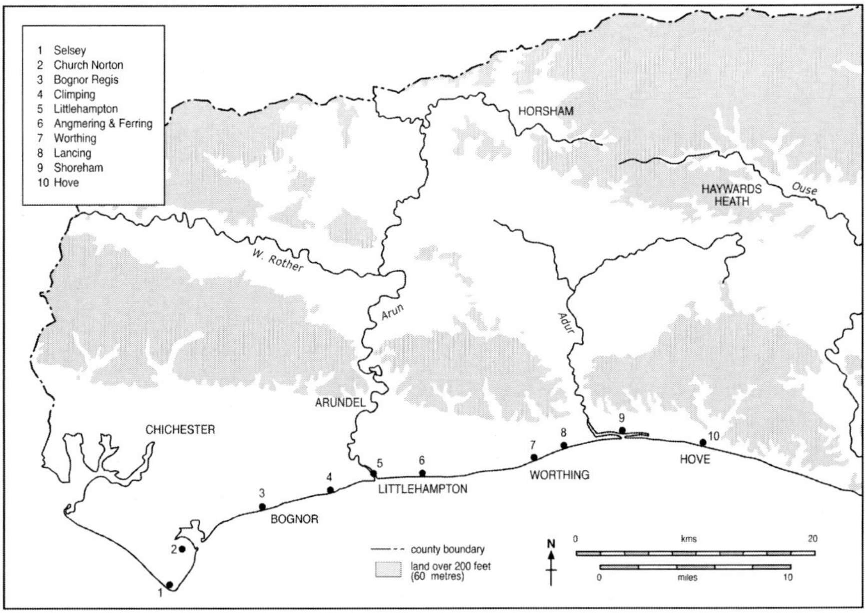

8 Map of coastal area, showing all of the sites covered in this chapter

Chichester Harbour is covered under the Chichester entry in Chapter 3 (Site 11), whilst Shoreham has two entries; the first in this chapter covers the coastal defences together with the town and its environs, whilst the airfield is covered in Chapter 4 (Site 37).

SITE 1: SELSEY

Period: **Tudor to the Second World War**
Type of Site: **Beach defences, pillboxes and sound mirror**

History

There is little evidence of any early fortification of the coast at Selsey, perhaps because much of the coastline has subsequently been lost to coastal erosion. A 1587 report on the Sussex Coast recommended that a fortification armed with a single demi-culverin and two sakers be built at Cakeham to the south of West Wittering. Cakeham Tower, built in 1519 by Bishop Sherborn, may have been used as a watchtower. Fire beacons were established at West Wittering, Bracklesham and Selsey in preparation for the arrival of the Spanish Armada.

A battery of three 36pdr cannon was established at East Beach, on the eastern side of Selsey Bill after 1796 (approx. SU868934) and, together with a smaller battery at Bognor, was intended to cover the sheltered anchorage known as 'The Park'. Wooden barracks were constructed to the rear of the battery in 1803, but had been demolished about 1812, with the battery disarmed at about the same time. The land on which the battery was located had been lost to coastal erosion by 1820. Admiralty signal posts were established at West Wittering and Selsey Bill in 1796.

During the First World War a sound mirror was constructed at Selsey (SZ 8636 9349). This concrete structure was designed to pick up the sound of incoming aircraft and airships from the east along the English Channel, but the introduction of faster aircraft in the 1930s made this form of early warning system obsolete.

The low-lying area of Selsey was particularly vulnerable to an enemy invasion force, although the numerous ditches and channels behind the beaches would have made progress inland difficult. To counter a landing in 1940, a line of anti-tank cubes set 18in apart were constructed at the top of the beach with barbed wire and scaffolding on the beach, whilst the REs laid both anti-tank and anti-personnel mines on the beach above the high water mark. Pillboxes and machine gun emplacements were built at regular intervals along the shoreline, and the Home Guard built defensive positions in the gardens of houses fronting the beach, whilst trenches were dug behind the sea wall at properties along Clayton Road and Seal Road.

A battery of 3.7in HAA guns was located on farmland at Medmerry, while other anti-aircraft guns were located on open ground at the east end of Seal Road and searchlights were positioned near Bill House. A HAA battery was also established

9 First World War sound mirror at Selsey. Now converted into a house, and registered as a Grade II listed building. The larger structure with the sloping roof at the rear of this picture is the upper part of the original sound mirror

just to the south of West Wittering, close to Cakeham Tower. An armoured train equipped with two 12pdr guns was deployed on the Selsey tramway. All of this may have been to no purpose other than to delay an invading force, as there was a plan to abandon Selsey and withdraw to the line of the Chichester Canal in the event of an invasion.

West Wittering became the location for a number of decoy sites during the war. The first was an airfield K/Q decoy site (No. 52) being set up for Thorney Island (see Site 30) at SZ770983, which became one of the most successful in terms of the number of Luftwaffe attacks it attracted until its closure in June 1942. In 1943, three Naval MQL decoy sites were established; No. 600 at Cobnor Point (SU791020), No. 601 at East Head (SZ765987) and No. 602 at Itchenor (SU784006). These were all established under Portsmouth Command with a command shelter and lighting set out to represent hards as part of the build up for the D-Day preparations.

The sites today

The sound mirror structure has been converted into a house and was registered as a Grade II listed building in 1999. The ground level around the house has been raised leaving part of the structure below ground, whilst the upper part has been divided into a number of rooms, thus making it difficult to recognise the structure as a sound mirror today (*9*).

A number of the anti-tank cubes survive around the coast at Selsey Bill, although coastal erosion and development has removed the majority. Single cubes still in their original locations are situated at SZ 8412 9342 and SZ 8426 9331 south of the West Sands Caravan Park, whilst others nearby are buried under the shingle bank. A group of broken-up cubes lie at the east end of the beach, close to an access ramp at SZ 8447 9304. Further west there are four cubes sitting across the shingle bank with at least one other partly buried (SZ 8343 9409). It is not clear whether these cubes are in situ, or have been moved to this position more recently. They do appear to be closing a gap between the beach and Broad Rife, which may have served as an anti-tank ditch covering the western approaches to Selsey. A further cube was situated further north along Broad Rife at SZ832941, suggesting that others originally lined the Rife, but this example could not be found in 2007.

Built into the bank of Broad Rife at SZ 8319 9462 and SZ 8319 9471 are two (of four previously recorded here) identical small square machine gun emplacements (*10*). Both emplacements have an embrasure facing west across the Rife with a large concrete table below for mounting the machine gun, and a second embrasure and protected entrance facing east (*colour plate 1*). Other pillboxes were located along the seafront, including one at the beach end of the footpath from the windmill at the West Sands Caravan Park (approx. SZ 8425 9325), but these were all removed soon after the war ended.

The control shelter for the Naval MQL decoy site No. 600 at Cobnor Point may still survive (approx. SU793023), although its associated generator building and lighting has now gone, and little survives of the other decoy sites.

A short distance offshore at Bracklesham Bay lies an almost intact but upside-down Landing Craft Tank, and nearby a Mulberry harbour bridge section, called a 'Whale'.

Directions and access

The sound mirror can be found by taking Beach Road from the B2145 in Selsey and following this until you reach the road junction just before the lake. The structure is situated in the middle of the road junction, looking very overgrown.

10 Machine gun emplacement built into the bank at Broad Rife at SZ 8319 9462, Selsey. The second emplacement can be seen 100m further along the bank

To find the defences along the coast and Broad Rife, follow the signposts to the West Sands Caravan Park from the centre of Selsey. The beach and in situ cubes can be reached by taking the footpath beside the windmill. After obtaining permission from the caravan park reception centre, it should be possible to drive along Medmerry Road to the entrance to the Environment Agency land. Park here, adjacent to the four cubes on the shingle bank, and follow the footpath that runs along the bank of Broad Rife to reach the two machine gun emplacements.

References/Background reading

Dobinson, C. 2000, *Fields of Deception*, London, Methuen Publishing Ltd
Fidler, C.J.M. 2000, *Selsey at War 1939-1945*, Selsey, Fidelity Processes
Hewitt, P. 2004, *Chichester Remembered*, Chichester, Phillimore & Co Ltd
McDonald, K. 1999, *Dive Sussex*, Teddington, Underwater World Publications Ltd
Mee, F. 1988, *A History of Selsey*, Chichester, Phillimore & Co Ltd

www.ajg41.clara.co.uk/mirrors/selsey.html

SITE 2: CHURCH NORTON

Period: **Tudor to the Second World War**
Type of site: **Battery and beach defences**

History

The Mound at Church Norton, adjacent to St Wilfrid's Chapel, probably originated as part of a small Norman castle in the eleventh century and had been abandoned just after 1100. At the time of the Armada a survey recommended the installation of defence works between Selsey and Littlehampton, and it is possible that the Mound may have been reused as a defensive earthwork. Other defensive works were located at East Norton, south of Church Norton, and on the east arm of Pagham Harbour, each armed with a single demi-culverin and two saker cannon. A fire beacon was also established at Pagham.

In 1796 an Admiralty signal station was established on the east side of the old entrance to Pagham Harbour.

In the early part of the Second World War, an anti-tank wall was constructed to the south of Church Norton (*11*). The concrete wall was some 2m high and 1m thick and stretched from Pagham Harbour at its north-east end (SZ 8733 9554) to a small lake at its south-west end, thus closing the only possible gap through which tanks could easily manoeuvre. Pillboxes were located around Pagham Harbour and other defences were placed to protect the roads leading inland, whilst the beach was protected by anti-tank cubes and barbed wire.

In 1942 an area of land (SZ865955) to the west of Church Norton was requisitioned for use as an ALG, known as RAF Selsey (see Site 32).

11 The anti-tank wall at Church Norton. The wall is 2m high and 1m thick, and has this stepped north-east end near Pagham Harbour

Pagham Harbour also became the location of a Naval MQL decoy site (No. 603) in 1943, with a command shelter and lighting set out to represent a hard as part of the build-up for D-Day (SZ866964). Mulberry harbour units were stored in preparation for D-Day by being sunk on the seabed off the coast between Selsey and Bognor Regis. One 'Phoenix A' unit was wrecked as it was being raised to the surface and now lies on the seabed some 3km off Pagham Harbour in 9m of water. A number of other Mulberry units were lost at that time, and in the same area are the remains of two 'D1' units, a 'C1' unit and a concrete petrol barge, together with a Landing Craft Infantry Mk 1 and a 'Cuckoo' (an RAF air sea rescue float that was moored off the coast to act as a refuge for downed pilots). After D-Day the wrecks off Pagham Harbour were used as targets by RAF Typhoons.

The sites today

The Mound at Church Norton survives today as a semi-circular earthwork comprising a bank some 2m high with an external ditch of similar depth and, although fenced off, can be viewed from the adjacent path (SZ872957). There are no visible remains of the other two Tudor defensive works.

The anti-tank wall survives, although there is little evidence for any of the other defensive works from the Second World War. A pillbox marked as 'uncertain' on a German map may survive in private woodland north of the wall (SZ873955), but it is possible that this has been mistaken, and may in fact have been the control building associated with a Sea Flame Barrage. Hidden in the woodland at this location are four partly sunken concrete tanks connected by a series of pipes, with the remains of a small building, probably the control/pump building, nearby. In the event of an invasion, fuel would have been pumped into the sea and/or Pagham Harbour from these tanks and set alight.

Two anti-tank buoys are located at the entrance to Norton Priory (SZ 8715 9561), and four white painted buoys have been placed at the entrance to the Trident Business Park (SZ 8605 9503) on the B2145 south of Norton. At Sidlesham there are the possible remains of a demolished Type 26 pillbox that would have covered the landing stage and beaches in the north-west corner of Pagham Harbour (SZ 8611 9729).

The Mulberry harbour units and other wrecks lying offshore can be visited by suitably equipped divers.

Directions and access

From the A27 at Chichester take the B2145 or B2201 towards Selsey. Turn off the B2145 on a minor road to Church Norton and follow this past the RAF Selsey plaque to the car park by the church. The Mound is situated beside the car park. To find the anti-tank wall walk down to the beach from the car park and turn right; it is located after 100m on the right, although a fence now prevents access. There is no access to the tanks and control building of the Sea Flame Barrage.

References/Background reading

Aldsworth, F.G. 1979, 'The Mound at Church Norton, Selsey and the site of St. Wilfred's Church', *Sussex Archaeological Collections* 117, 103-7

Aldsworth, F.G. & Garnett, E.D. 1981, 'Excavations on 'The Mound' at Church Norton, Selsey, in 1911 and 1965', *Sussex Archaeological Collections* 119, 217-221

Dobinson, C. 2000, *Fields of Deception*, London, Methuen Publishing Ltd

Mace, M.F. 1997, *Sussex Wartime Relics and Memorials*, Storrington, Historic Military Press

McDonald, K. 1999, *Dive Sussex*, Teddington, Underwater World Publications Ltd

SITE 3: BOGNOR REGIS

Period: **Second World War**
Type of Site: **Beach defences, Coastal batteries and Pillboxes**

History

Although Pagham Harbour had been defended at the time of the Spanish Armada, it was not until the Napoleonic Wars that a battery was set up at Bognor. Two 36pdr cannon were placed in a battery in the vicinity of Barn Rocks and, along with the larger battery at Selsey, covered the sheltered anchorage known as 'The Park'. Barracks were established at Aldwick (approx. SZ913988) and Bognor (approx. SZ935995), although both were abandoned after 1815. An Admiralty signal station was established to the east of Bognor in 1795, but was lost to coastal erosion, a replacement being built at Middleton-on-Sea in 1804.

The Norman Thompson Flight Company had begun life as the White and Thompson aircraft plant in 1910 at Middleton-on-Sea. During the First World

War it undertook the design and manufacture of flying boats, and built some 300 aircraft, including some under contract for other manufacturers. Financial problems led to receivers being appointed in 1918, and the company was acquired by Handley-Page Ltd in 1919.

In 1940, the seafront at Bognor was placed into a state of defence with barbed wire entanglements and anti-tank cubes placed along the promenade, whilst the beaches were mined and scaffolding was erected at the low tide mark. The pier, which opened in 1865 and had a landing stage to be used by paddle steamers added in 1903, had its central section blown up to stop it being used as a landing stage by the enemy; it was used by the Royal Navy as an OP under the name of HMS Barbara. Type 26 pillboxes were constructed at regular intervals along the promenade to cover the beach. Bognor Regis was established as a coastal town Nodal Point, and further pillboxes and machine gun emplacements were located to the north of the town at North Bersted. There was also an anti-tank ditch about 15ft deep around the west and north of North Bersted towards Felpham Rife, and roadblocks with concrete blocks and hairpin rails were placed across the roads, including one on the A259 at The Royal Oak public house, which was covered by a pillbox.

An ECB equipped with two 5.5in BL Mk I guns and two searchlights was established in 1941. The battery was organised as two separate sections (left and right) and was initially manned by 149 Coast Battery of 553 Coast Regiment, with the battery HQ being located in a hotel in Aldwick Avenue. Four machine guns were later added for anti-aircraft defence. The Right Section was located in a garden on the seaward side of Aldwick Avenue (SZ 9203 9850) and faced south, whilst the Left Section was located further east at Felpham. It had a magazine at the rear, a searchlight and a two-storey command and OP. From 1942 the battery was manned by the Home Guard.

Felpham was also the home of the Royal Navy School of Photography, with houses being requisitioned between Limmer Lane and Fourth Avenue.

The civil defence organisations were kept busy during the war with numerous air raids on the town. Surface air-raid shelters were erected around the town, including two in the High Street, whilst the entrance to the Town Hall was bricked up for use as a 22-person capacity shelter.

An airfield night decoy site (Q51(b)) for Tangmere was established at Colworth (SU926027) north of Bognor in1940, whilst a temporary Starfish decoy site (TSF76) for Chichester was also set up at Colworth (SU927034) in June 1942 as a result of the Baedecker raids. An ALG was constructed on flat ground to the north-west of Bognor in early 1943 (see Site 32).

The sites today

Nothing survives of the earlier defence sites, although the location of the Norman Thompson Flight Company was marked by the survival of some of its buildings until they were demolished to make way for housing in 1997.

Few of the fixed defences along the seafront survive at Bognor, with all of the pillboxes and other obstructions removed at the end of the war, although some of the cubes were incorporated into the base of the sea wall and promenade. A single anti-tank cube can be seen in the rear of the sea wall at SZ 9486 9923.

Surprisingly, however, some of the Right Section position of the ECB can still be discerned amongst the seafront buildings off Aldwick Avenue (*12*). The location of the gun position is marked by the distinctive concrete lip at the front of the gun floor, whilst a small concrete building on its east side may be a war shelter or shell store. To the east of this gun position is a searchlight post, added to an existing building in 1941, with the front part of the structure supported on stilts, and now converted into a beach hut (*colour plate 2*). On the west side of the gun positions is a single-storey concrete building with a shuttered opening on the seaward side, and also now used as a beach hut. This may be another battery building. The battery OP is situated in a purpose-built tower that was added to the seaward side of the house immediately behind the gun position and has now been fully incorporated into the house.

The gun post of the Left Section at Felpham was converted into a hacienda-like house in the 1980s and can be found at the end of Clyde Road adjacent to the promenade (SZ 9489 9928). The gun post is at ground level and has been incorporated into the house as the master bedroom. Next door to this building is another house, which may have been converted from the OP and searchlight buildings. A ramp onto the promenade at the end of Outram Road has three anti-tank hairpin rail sockets, with another four concrete patches that originally may have also been sockets (SZ 9487 9926).

At North Bersted there are a number of surviving defence positions along the line of a stream. The first is a unique partly sunken pillbox (SU 9231 0157); very narrow with two main machine gun embrasures facing north-west, and a single smaller embrasure along each short wall. There is an external blast wall protecting the entrance. An extension, resembling an infantry section post with four rifle loopholes and an external loopholed blast wall, has been added to the rear of the pillbox to cover the approach from the south. Nearby is a rather poorly designed infantry section post (SU 9251 0159) with a long loopholed wall. Further east is a Type 24 pillbox (SU 9262 0160) covering the Shripney Lane Bridge. Another Type 24 pillbox may survive in a garden nearby, and although the anti-tank ditch was in-filled after the war, it has recently been rediscovered during an archaeological evaluation.

The civil defence structures in Bognor Regis were removed at the end of the war. The covered entrance to the Town Hall (SZ 9383 9903) is still present, but there is no evidence surviving for the brickwork that filled the gaps to form the air-raid shelter.

Directions and access

The anti-tank cube incorporated into the sea wall can be found by walking down Sea Road on the east side of Butlins holiday centre, climbing the steps onto the sea

12 Site of the right hand section of the Bognor Emergency Coastal Battery at Aldwick. The gun position is marked by the concrete structure in the foreground, with a war shelter or engine room behind the white wall on the right. Beyond that on stilts is the converted searchlight post, whilst the observation post is built into the house behind the gun position

wall/promenade, turning left and walking to the corner, where it can be seen at ground level at the rear of the wall. The buildings adapted from the Felpham Left Section of the ECB are a short distance further along the promenade between Outram Road and Clyde Road, along with the hairpin rail sockets.

To see the remains of the Aldwick Right Section of the ECB, park at the west end of Marine Drive and walk along the beach to the west parallel with Aldwick Avenue; all of the structures are on private property, but can be seen from the beach.

The North Bersted pillboxes are located to the north of North Bersted Street and Shripney Lane, but are all on private farmland and cannot be visited.

References/Background reading

Dobinson, C. 2000, *Fields of Deception*, London, Methuen Publishing Ltd

Jones, G. & Dunkin, D. 2000, *An Archaeological Desk-based Assessment and Walkover Survey at Land to the North of North Bersted, West Sussex*, Ditchling, Archaeology South-East

Mace, M.F. 1997, *Sussex Wartime Relics and Memorials*, Storrington, Historic Military Press

Martin, R.G. 1996, *Pillbox at SU923015, North Bersted, Bognor Regis, West Sussex* (Drawing)

Saunders, A. 1995, *Bognor at War*, Midhurst, Middleton Press

PRO WO 166/11008

1940/11/20 Sudostkuste England: Schragbildreihe IV

SITE 4: CLIMPING

Period: Second World War
Type of Site: Beach defences and gun emplacements

History

Atherington Beach at Climping is a low-lying shingle beach between Littlehampton and Bognor Regis and would have made an ideal landing place for any prospective enemy. In 1587 it was recommended that trenches be dug to defend the beaches at nearby Middleton and Elmer for musket-armed militia. Towers for mounting light artillery at Middleton and Atherington were proposed in the 1870s, but nothing came of this. It was only the threat of a German invasion in 1940 that prompted the building of more substantial beach defences here.

A 2ft-thick concrete anti-tank wall was built along the rear of the beach extending from TQ 0043 0069 to TQ 0112 0091. Concrete anti-tank cubes were placed in a line along the top of the beach and extended eastwards from Atherington to Littlehampton (Site 5), and west to Bognor Regis (Site 3). These defences were backed up by barbed wire, minefields and beach scaffolding, together with pillboxes and other prepared positions.

Later in the war, the beach was used for D-Day landing rehearsals. One participant recorded that 'the mines and steel anti-invasion obstacles had been cleared away, except for those at the very top of the beach'.

A couple of miles inland from the beach was Ford airfield (Site 36), which was subjected to a number of air attacks during the Battle of Britain. A HAA battery was located to the south of Climping village, with another further north at Ford. The school at Climping was provided with a 50-person surface air-raid shelter, whilst at Tortington another surface air-raid shelter was built in the grounds of the college, which was used as a hospital during the war.

Just to the east of Ford Station, the railway line crosses the River Arun, and then divides three ways at Arundel Junction 500m beyond. This was obviously an important strategic location and potential crossing point, as two gun emplacements were built to cover the railway bridge, and equipped with 18pdr field guns.

The sites today

At least 180 anti-tank cubes survive at the rear of the anti-tank wall at Atherington beach, of which 112 are positioned at the rear of the anti-tank wall in the car park TQ 0069 0081 (*13*). They continue further west to TQ 0043 0069 where a dump of concrete may be evidence for other demolished defence installations. East of the car park another 43 cubes line the rear of the sea wall, with a further 25 located around the track to The Mill. It is possible that some of the evenly spaced cubes at the rear of the wall may be in their original positions, but most have obviously been moved to their current location, perhaps during the clearance of beach obstacles for the D-Day landing rehearsals. No pillboxes survive on this stretch of coastline, but

13 Anti-tank cubes behind the sea wall at Atherington Beach, Climping

there is evidence for a prepared position at the east end of Atherington beach (TQ 0112 0091). This comprises a section of wall to which an additional foot of height has been added in concrete, into which four loopholes have been incorporated (*14*). These loopholes would have allowed soldiers sheltering behind the wall to fire onto the beach without exposing themselves

The gun emplacements at Ford Station are constructed from concrete and are open-backed with a large embrasure to take a field gun. The first gun emplacement is located on the west side of the River Arun in the edge of a field at TQ 0028

14 Loopholed wall at Atherington Beach, Climping (TQ 0112 0091)

0415, facing east towards the railway bridge and Arundel Junction. The second emplacement is on the east side of the river in a tree line at TQ008041, 150 yards east of the railway bridge and to the north of Arundel Junction. It is facing west and also covers the railway bridge. There are no other surviving pillboxes or defensive positions in the vicinity of these two emplacements. Adjacent to the railway bridge in a small compound at TQ004041 are two small Nissen huts.

The surface air-raid shelter at Climping School was located at TQ 0043 0176, and comprised a rectangular brick building with a concrete roof. There was an original door on one long side close to the south end and four air vents along the top of the same wall. Although the shelter was used as a storeroom until recently, it was unfortunately demolished in August 2007.

Directions and access

The beach defences at Atherington can be found by turning off the A259 into Climping Street, signposted to Climping beach. Follow this to the car park at the end. There is a charge for parking. A short walk east along the public footpath on the beach takes you past a continuation of the sea wall, now largely buried by shingle, to the section of wall with the loopholes.

To find the gun emplacements, take Ford Road south from Arundel, and cross over the level crossing at Ford Station. Pull into a layby on the left just after the junction with Ford Lane. Follow the footpath east past the chapel to Ford Marina, and then continue along the river embankment north towards the railway bridge. Just before reaching the bridge, the first emplacement can be seen in the field edge on the left. A distant view of the second emplacement can be gained from the north side of the bridge. Both emplacements are on private land.

References/Background reading

Goodwin, J.E. 1985, *The Military Defence of West Sussex*, Midhurst, Middleton Press
Defence of Britain database (http://www.pillboxesuk.co.uk)

SITE 5: LITTLEHAMPTON

Period: **Tudor to the Second World War**
Type of Site: **Battery, fort and Nodal Point**

History

The first defences for Littlehampton, or Arundel Haven as it was then known, were probably constructed about 1587 when it was recommended that a fort armed with two demi-culverins and two sakers be sited on the east bank of the River Arun. The fort was probably constructed of earthen ramparts with fascines and gabions to form a parapet, behind which the cannon were placed on a wooden platform. If constructed, the fort was short-lived, as it is not mentioned in a survey of forts and batteries made in 1652-4. The next fortification to be built was a five-gun battery, which is shown on a Board of Ordnance map of 1736. The battery was situated on the east side of the river adjacent to Hampton West Mill and may have covered an old river course, it thus became obsolete when the new harbour entrance was cut in 1735-36.

A new battery was built in the 1760s and was once again located on the east side of the river, covering the new harbour entrance. This bastion battery had turf ramparts around the gun platform, with the master gunner's house, magazine, stables and storehouse located to its rear, all surrounded by a stockade fence. The battery was initially armed with seven 18pdr cannon, although this appears to have increased to some 10 cannon by 1801, when it was suggested they be replaced by captured French 36pdrs. At this time the battery was in poor condition and it is not clear whether it was repaired, however 200 troops were ordered to Littlehampton to support the battery. By the mid nineteenth century the battery was obsolete and it was dismantled and sold off for use as a coastguard station.

A new fort was built on the west side of the harbour entrance in 1854, and comprised a lunette-shaped rampart with a dry ditch at its front and sides (*1*). It was similar to the fort at Shoreham, which was constructed a few years later (Site 9). In the centre of the ditch was a brick and flint Carnot wall, loopholed along its length, and at the corners there were open bastions, also loopholed, to provide flanking fire along the front face of the wall. The gun platform mounted three 68pdr guns and two 32pdr guns, with two large underground magazines and four recesses for shell storage. Located at the rear of the fort was a brick defensible barrack block accommodating the garrison of 50 officers and men, with the open ends of the ditch closed with a loopholed wall. There were additional earthworks protecting the rear of the fort pierced by a curving entrance passage which was flanked with brick walls; a hut outside the fort accommodated a further 30 infantry. Within 20 years of its construction, ordnance technology had moved on and the fort was deemed inadequate in both construction and armament, and in need of modernisation. Taken out of service in 1873, the guns were removed in 1891 and the fort was dismantled by 1900, having been employed in its final years as a barracks for the troops using the nearby rifle range.

In 1940, the beach defences continued from Climping along West Beach to the mouth of the River Arun and then along the seafront at Littlehampton. Concrete anti-tank cubes were placed in a line along the top of the beach and were backed up by barbed wire, minefields and beach scaffolding together with pillboxes. Littlehampton became a coastal town Nodal Point with roadblocks set up at entry points into the town and other defensive positions established. The anti-tank cubes were built in situ along the edge of the promenade and between houses to block gaps. One line of cubes ran along the north side of Cornwall Road and another row was built in Meadow Way, together with a 15ft deep tank trap. Beach huts were filled with shingle and used as roadblocks, whilst hairpin rails were used to block roads around the edge of the town. The pillboxes along the promenade were disguised; one at the bottom end of Sea Lane had large painted windows to make it look like a seafront kiosk, whilst a Type 26 pillbox on the shore at Harsfold Road had a pitched roof and was painted to look like a house. The Home Guard had their HQ in East Street School and manned trenches near the base of the lighthouse, with other posts at the Arun View public house covering the bridge over the River Arun, at 'Thorncroft' near the cemetery, and at the fort on West Beach.

A pillbox positioned close to the beach and the mouth of the river contained a control switch that would sink a blockship, which was intended to block the river and put the swing bridge out of use. A boom was also positioned to block the river mouth, with its winch on the west bank, possibly in the fort.

An ECB equipped with two 6in BL Mk II guns and two searchlight posts manned by 344 Battery of 553 (later 521) Coast Regiment was set up on the green in front of the Beach Hotel in South Terrace. The battery OP was in the coastguard lookout tower on the promenade, and the gun positions were disguised as bungalows. A number of anti-aircraft guns were positioned in the town, including one on top of Sparks warehouse and another on the roof of ARC Marine.

At Lyminster, north of Littlehampton, loopholes were cut through garden walls covering the road to Arundel, whilst a machine gun post was set up in the garden of 'Churchfields' overlooking the flat ground behind the church. The Pavilion School was turned into a stronghold surrounded by barbed wire after the children had all been evacuated.

The ARP HQ was located at 'Groombridge', with wardens' posts there and at five other locations in the town. A single storey building north of the council depot off Harwood Road became the ARP depot. Initially there were six public air-raid shelters, including trench shelters and basements, with the private shelter at the Norfolk Laundry also being used as a public shelter at night. In June 1940 another nine public shelters, mostly surface shelters, were constructed and air-raid shelters were also built at the schools. The First Aid Post was situated in the Masonic Hall in Church Street. The Auxiliary Fire Service had a number of posts across the town and also manned a fireboat in the harbour.

The boat building yards of David Hillyard Ltd and William Osborne Ltd, on the west bank of the River Arun at Littlehampton, were involved in producing coastal craft such as Motor Torpedo Boats, Motor Launches and Air Sea Rescue Launches, and later in the war, landing craft.

The sites today

Nothing survives today of the earliest fortifications at Littlehampton, although the 1760 battery on the east bank survives as a large rectangular mound within the amusement park (TQ 0285 0136).

On the west bank parts of the nineteenth-century fort survive behind the dunes of West Beach (TQ 0270 0118). Although very overgrown (*colour plate 3*), the ramparts, Carnot wall and corner bastions can be seen from the adjacent path, where there is an information board describing the fort. The barracks were demolished in the 1960s, but a War Department boundary marker post can be seen from the West Beach car park in the grounds of the golf course to the north of the fort (approx. TQ 0274 0126).

The nineteenth-century rifle range was located on the west side of the golf course, centred on TQ 0255 0130 and, according to the 1899 OS map, comprised a series of firing points heading northwards out to 800 yards, with the targets at the top of the beach.

The Second World War defences have mostly been removed, with over 400 anti-tank cubes being removed from the golf course and West Beach alone. There is no trace surviving of the ECB (located at approx. TQ 0300 0133) although part of the coastguard lookout tower on the promenade (TQ 0290 0133) may have been used as the OP, but this does not match the wartime photograph of the battery OP. None of the pillboxes have survived, although on West Beach there is a concrete structure overlooking the beach that may have been an OP (TQ 0279 0117). It comprises a small rectangular concrete structure, with a bricked-up embrasure in its south-east corner, that sits on top of a larger concrete bunker, now buried by the sand dunes.

Two groups of sockets for hairpin rails that would have formed parts of roadblocks blocking the northern entry points into Littlehampton still survive today. The first group are at the junction of Arundel Road and Kent Road (TQ 0271 0262) and the second group is at the entrance to Townsend Crescent (TQ 0355 0283). In each case some 40 sockets for the hairpin rails can be seen in the original concrete road surface (*15*). It is likely that other groups may survive, but are now covered by modern tarmac resurfacing. The Arun View public house still exists on the east side of the bridge, although there is no surviving evidence for

15 Anti-tank hairpin rail sockets in the road surface at the entrance to Townsend Crescent, Littlehampton (TQ 0355 0283)

the associated roadblock at the bridge. A little further north along Bridge Road 16 anti-tank cylinders are located at the entrance to Quayside (TQ 0205 0238).

North of Littlehampton, on the main road (A284) to Arundel, there are two groups of loopholes at the village of Lyminster. The first group are on a sharp corner at the junction with Church Lane (TQ 0249 0476), and comprise three square-cut loopholes, two at shoulder height and one close to the ground, all facing south covering the approach from Littlehampton. Further north on the A284, two angled loopholes are cut into the south-east and north-east corners of a brick and flint garden wall on a long straight section of road (TQ 0285 0552).

Directions and access

The surviving mound of the 1760 battery can be found in the amusement park behind the coastguard lookout tower on the east side of the river. To find the first group of hairpin rail sockets, take the B2187 (Horsham Road) turning off into Horsham Road West, then into Hill Road with Townsend Crescent being first on the right. The second group is off the A284 (Arundel Road) at the junction with Kent Road immediately after a sharp left-hand corner. Continue along the A284 to Lyminster to find the loopholed walls. The first loopholes are in the wall of Lyminster House at the junction between the A284 and Church Lane. Turn into Church Lane to park. The second group are in the wall of Brook Lawn on the west side of the A284. There is no parking at this second site.

To get to the fort and other sites on the west bank of the River Arun, take the B2187 (Terminus Road), passing the Arun View and the anti-tank cylinders at Quayside on the way, to join the A259 at the roundabout, and follow the A259 towards Bognor. Turn first left after crossing the river and follow Ferry Road to the pay and display car park at West Beach. The concrete OP is immediately behind the café at West Beach, whilst the fort can be found a short way along the path beside the café. There is no access to the fort itself.

References/Background reading

Cooper, G.R. 2001, *& Hitler Stopped Play*, Cambridge, Vanguard Press
Crook, P. 1998, *Sussex Home Guard*, Midhurst, Middleton Press
Goodwin, J.E. 1985 *The Military Defence of West Sussex*, Midhurst, Middleton Press
Jones, I. 1989, *Wartime Littlehampton*, Arun District Council
Jones, I. 1995, *Wartime Littlehampton 1941-1945*, Littlehampton Local History Society
Thompson, H.J.F. 1978, *Littlehampton Through The Wars*, Littlehampton Printers

SITE 6: ANGMERING AND FERRING

Period: **First and Second World Wars**
Type of Site: **Landing Ground and coastal defences**

History

A landing ground was opened in 1917 between Rustington and East Preston villages. In 1918 it became a training depot station for the USAAS, with grass runways that ran north to south along the current line of Sea Avenue. It was equipped with six large aeroplane sheds, each capable of taking a Handley Page 0/400, together with workshops, repair sheds and accommodation buildings. The construction of the airfield was completed just as the war finished and the buildings were quickly disposed of (some of the hangars were sold to Osborne's, a boat builder in Littlehampton, and rebuilt in River Road) and the land was relinquished in 1919.

In the summer of 1940, the beaches from East Preston to Ferring were put into a state of defence as elsewhere along the West Sussex coast. The defences included anti-tank cubes, which were placed along the top of the beach, together with barbed wire, minefields, beach scaffolding and pillboxes. An ECB was established at East Preston in 1940, initially comprising a single 4in BL Mk 9 gun, which was mounted in a casemate and manned by 69 Medium Regiment Royal Artillery (RA). This gun was later used as a flanking gun when the battery received two 6" guns and two searchlights in 1941, and was then manned by the 346 Battery of 553 Coast Regiment, who had their HQ and billets in the Blue Peter Club. Angmering also became a coastal town Nodal Point.

The sites today

The site of the First World War airfield (centred on TQ059020) has now been built over, and although most of the buildings were removed after the war, two

16 Type 26 pillbox at Ferring incorporated into the sea wall (TQ 0987 0152). It has embrasures on three sides and an entrance to the rear, but is now bricked up and rendered

still remain. The first is the original guardhouse ('Fairholm' in Sea Avenue TQ 0584 0255), which stands at the original entrance to the airfield adjacent to the B2140, and has been converted into a residence. The second is apparently a former salvage shed that has been converted into a bungalow ('Nortons' in Preston Avenue TQ 0559 0238).

The Second World War beach defences were cleared after the end of the war, although locals can remember the beach scaffolding remaining in place for a short while after the war. A single Type 26 pillbox at Ferring is the only surviving element of the beach defences (TQ 0987 0152) on this stretch of the coast. It has embrasures on three sides and an entrance to the rear, but has been bricked up and rendered, and is now incorporated into the sea wall (*16*). When recently opened up, it was found to have one of its wooden tables still in situ. It has now been re-sealed and a plaque placed on its side.

There appears to be a significant part of the ECB surviving between the beach and South Strand. Emerging onto the beach from Sea Road, the first structure to be seen is a beach kiosk, which may have originated as a military building. Walking east past the dinghy park there is a searchlight post now used as a beach house (TQ 0725 0150) (*colour plate 4*) and a little further on is the distinctive tall square shape of an OP that has been added onto the end of a house ('Pergolas'). Beside this house, and fronting a formal garden, is the first gun floor (TQ 0739 0149), marked by the concrete lip at the front of the gun floor. A little further east, past two more houses, is a second gun floor (TQ 0746 0148), again with the concrete lip now marking the end of the garden. The house behind this gun floor (Marine House) also appears to have an OP built into it and on the east side of the gun floor is a small building, now used as a garage, but perhaps originally an engine room or store (TQ 0747 0151). It is possible that this second gun position is actually the location of the 4in flank battery.

Directions and access

The surviving airfield buildings are hidden in the maze of private roads at Rustington. Turn into Sea Avenue from the B2140 (Station Road); 'Fairholm' is the first building on the right. Continue down Sea Avenue and at the first junction turn into Preston Avenue, continue along here to find 'Nortons' on the right at the junction with The Bramblings.

To find the Type 26 pillbox at Ferring, park at the west end of Marine Drive and walk along Pattersons Walk for about 100m; the pillbox is in the sea wall on the left.

From the A259 take the B2140 to East Preston, follow the maze of roads through the housing estates until you get to Sea Road, which should be followed until the parade of shops at the junction with South Strand is reached. Park in Sea Road or Seaview Road, not in South Strand as you may end up being clamped! Walk to the end of Sea Road and onto the beach and turn left to find the surviving elements of the ECB, which are all on private property, but can be seen from the beach.

References/Background reading

Ashworth, R.C.B. 1985, *Action Stations 9. Military airfields of the Central South and South-East*, Wellingborough, Patrick Stephens Ltd

Mace, M.F. 2007, 'Wartime Pillbox Re-opened', *Britain at War Magazine*, No. 3, Green Arbor Publishing Ltd, 7

Thompson, H.J.F. 1978, *Littlehampton Through The Wars*, Littlehampton Printers

SITE 7: WORTHING

Period: **First and Second World Wars**
Type of Site: **Beach defences, coastal battery and civil defence sites**

History

At the end of the nineteenth century and up to the First World War, the Downs to the north of Worthing had been used by volunteer units for their annual training camps (see also Findon; Site 19). During the First World War, numerous hutted and tented camps sprang up around Worthing to accommodate the troops in training and waiting to be moved across the Channel to France. It was also planned to build a training depot station for the USAAS at Goring-by-Sea (approx. TQ114036) north of the Chichester to Brighton railway line. The 168-acre site would have had hangars, a repair shed and hutted accommodation, but the end of the war meant that construction was stopped and the airfield was never used.

17 The seafront on the east side of Worthing in 1940, looking west along the promenade. Note the single line of anti-tank cubes, the large gun emplacement on the beach at Splash Point, and the gap in Worthing Pier. *West Sussex County Council Library Service: PP/WSL/WGP00043*. www.westsussexpast.org.uk/pictures

As with all the other south coast towns, Worthing was put into a state of defence in 1940 as a Nodal Point. A single line of anti-tank cubes, constructed by local civilian firms, lined the promenade, whilst barbed wire and mines were laid on the beach (*17*). On either side of the town anti-tank scaffolding was erected on the open ground to the rear of the beach. A gap was blown in the pier, and the beach huts were removed and filled with shingle for use as roadblocks. Pillboxes were constructed at intervals along Marine Parade and West Parade, including a unique example on the beach at the south end of George V Avenue. A gun emplacement was built on the beach at Splash Point to the east of the pier and the Lido was fortified with sandbagged positions.

Other pillboxes and defensive positions were placed to cover roads from the seafront leading inland, including a Type 26 pillbox, given the nickname 'Hyam Already', which was positioned on the roundabout in front of the Town Hall, and a machine gun post in Shaftesbury Avenue to cover the bridge over the railway line. There were also sunken machine gun emplacements covered with turf, which were placed on Findon Golf Course to the north of the town. Some machine gun posts were improvised, comprising sandbagged positions with wood and corrugated iron behind loopholed walls. Worthing was ringed with anti-tank cubes in the surrounding countryside, stretching out to Durrington Hill and along the Arundel Road to Cemetery Corner, where a pillbox was located on the south side of the cemetery, and as far north as the Findon Road. Roadblocks were erected at all the entry points into this defensive perimeter.

An ECB was set up on a grass strip at the bottom of Grand Avenue. Initially the two 6in BL Mk II guns (originally from HMS Lion) were placed in sandbagged positions, but these were later replaced by brick casemates with a concrete roof, which were disguised a beachfront buildings (*3*). The battery position was enclosed with barbed wire and a magazine was placed in a garden to the rear of the guns, together with at least one Nissen hut. A house at the corner of Grand Avenue and West Parade was requisitioned as the command post and OP, and there was an engine room located nearby. A hole was cut through the solid south wall of a block of flats in Marine Parade for use as an OP. There were also two searchlights, with a field gun added in 1941 and two 20mm anti-aircraft guns in 1942. The guns were initially manned by 345 Battery of 553 Coast Regiment and then from 1942 by members of the 5th Sussex (Worthing) Home Guard Battalion.

The civil defence preparations for Worthing appear to have been dogged by controversy. Initially trench shelters were to be constructed throughout the town, but these only had capacity for 6000 people (10 per cent of the population). It was then decided that trench shelters would not be built at schools, but at nearby recreation grounds, although eventually surface shelters were also built at the schools. Covered trench shelters were constructed at 14 locations.

Worthing public air-raid shelters

Location of Shelter	**Capacity (people)**
Beach House Park	638
Broadwater Green	314
Durrington Housing Estate	314
Gloucester Place	280
Homefield Park	638
Manor Sports Ground	638
Mulberry Lane Depot	314
Offington Corner (Cemetery land)	314
Steyne Gardens	638
Stoke Abbott Road	314
Tarring Recreation Ground	638
Victoria Park	638
West Park	314
Winton Place	150

There were also a number of surface shelters in the town, with an additional 16 surface shelters being built in the central shopping area in 1943. These later surface shelters appear to have been similar to Stanton shelters with a curved roof and blast walls at each end; some of these were also built at schools. The ARP Headquarters was located in the Town Hall, with wardens' posts built at locations around the town, and Beach House was used a store for gas masks and for training. The Observer Corps post was situated on the roof of the Southern Pavilion.

A GCI station was established on the outskirts of Worthing as RAF Durrington in 1941 and was the first to become operational in England. Housing development had been planned in the area and a network of roads had been built before work stopped on the outbreak of war. Initially it was a mobile unit, but this was replaced with hutted accommodation, and then in 1942 a Happidrome operations block was built. To disguise its purpose, the building was camouflaged as a barn using timber and sheeting. There were no air-raid shelters built although there was apparently an underground workshop, and the 'reserve' (a backup site in case the main site was knocked out) was located in the house opposite the main entrance. The domestic site was located at Field Place, with WAAFs billeted in houses in Shaftesbury Road and Bolsover Road.

Highdown Hill to the north-west of Worthing had been used as a beacon site at the time of the Spanish Armada (1587) and although it had been made a Scheduled Ancient Monument in 1930, a radar station was built on the hill during the Second World War. A large hole was excavated in the centre of the Late Bronze Age hilltop enclosure to take the generator, whilst a number of slit trenches and machine gun posts were dug around its perimeter. The radar was originally an Army CD No. 1 Mk. 1 type, but was later taken over and upgraded by the RAF.

The sites today

The defences and civil defence structures were quickly removed at the end of the war (*6*) and very little remains in the town to be seen today. The ECB at the end of Grand Avenue was located at the top of the steps onto the promenade (TQ 1336 0204). The house at the corner of Grand Avenue and West Parade that was requisitioned as the CP and OP is still there, but nothing can be seen of the modifications that were made to it, whilst the flats in Marine Parade have had a modern extension added to the southern end. None of the pillboxes or gun emplacements have survived along the seafront at Worthing, although metal reinforcement rods occasionally appear through the shingle on the beach at the end of Sea Lane (TQ 113018) where a pillbox was located. There are three loopholes in a wall on the corner of Brougham Road (TQ 1684 0320) that runs north from the seafront on the east side of Worthing. The loopholes have been blocked with a different coloured type of brick, and are positioned to cover the approaching road from the seafront (*colour plate 5*).

A number of air-raid shelters still exist around the town. A trench shelter located in the north-east corner of Broadwater Green (*18*) can be made out due to the distinctive bump in the ground (TQ 1437 0463). The entrance originally faced Ardsheal Road, but can no longer be seen, however six of the original eight emergency exit covers are visible on the top of the bump. Another trench shelter is located below the car park at the end of Winton Place (TQ 1467 0303). An overgrown surface shelter, now used as a store, sits in the churchyard of St Botolph Church (TQ 1378 0285).

The RAF Durrington GCI station building is still in use today, albeit much altered, as part of a special needs school in Palatine Road (TQ 1177 0404). The building has had a new entrance and windows added (*19*), and recently a large extension located on its east side. However, the outline of the original Happidrome

18 This trench air-raid shelter located in the north-east corner of Broadwater Green, can be made out due to the distinctive bump in the ground (TQ 1437 0463)

19 The RAF Durrington GCI station Happidrome building is still in use today, albeit much altered, as part of a special needs school in Palatine Road, Worthing

has been preserved and many of the features of its original structure can be seen, including the boiler rooms with their water towers and inside a ladies toilet still has its original layout and fittings. Also of interest are the weakened bonding lines in the brickwork of the building, which were presumably to provide blow-out areas in the event of the structure being hit by a bomb, thus providing a means of escape for those inside. Field Place is now part of a sport and arts complex (TQ 1220 0352) and has a number of underground rooms (now blocked up), although stories of an extensive network of tunnels should be treated with caution.

Directions and access

The site of the ECB was at the south end of Grand Avenue, where some steps up onto the esplanade mark its position. With your back to the sea the flats in which the OP was located are on the left side of Grand Avenue and the CP/OP is on the right corner. The loopholes can be found by turning into Broughton Road from the Brighton Road (A259) and are located at the first corner.

The surviving air-raid shelter in the south-east corner of Broadwater Green off the A24 into Worthing, is at the junction with Ardsheal Road. Winton Place is close to the town's museum, whilst the surface shelter at St. Botolph Church is in Landsdown Road off Heene Road.

To find the GCI building, turn off the A2032 (Littlehampton Road) into The Boulevard and then turn right into Palatine Road at the first roundabout. The school is a short distance along this road on the right, but there is no access without making prior arrangements. Field Place is off the next roundabout south along The Boulevard.

References/Background reading

Clark, C. & Taylor, R. 1989, *Worthing at War*, Eastbourne, Beckett Features

Crook, P. 1998, *Sussex Home Guard*, Midhurst, Middleton Press

Downer, K. 1979, *Worthing in Wartime 1939-1945*, Worthing Library: S WOR 900

Goodwin, J.E. 1985, *The Military Defence of West Sussex*, Midhurst, Middleton Press

Mace, M.F. 1996, *Frontline Sussex: The Defence Lines of West Sussex 1939-1945*, Storrington, Historic Military Press

Mace, M.F. 2002, 'A Suitable Disguise: Camouflage Officers at Work in Sussex', Aldis No. 71, *UK Fortifications Club*

White, S. 2000, *Worthing Past*, Chichester, Phillimore & Co. Ltd

Undated Logbook: ARP Wardens Post No. 4 OQ Worthing 1940-41, Worthing Library: S WOR 900

1952 *Signals: Volume V, Fighter Control and Interception, The Second World War 1939-1945*, Royal Air Force, Air Ministry

SITE 8: LANCING

Period: **Second World War**
Type of site: **Beach defences and air-raid shelters**

History

The anti-tank cubes and associated barbed wire, beach scaffolding and mines continued along the coast at Lancing, where the shingle beach would have made an ideal landing place. Pillboxes were constructed at regular intervals at the top of the beach, often being built into the sea wall or designed to blend into the shoreline landscape. A HAA battery was located to the north of the A259 at

Lancing Beach, probably as part of the defences for Shoreham Airfield (Site 37). There were six 3.7in HAA guns positioned in circular concrete emplacements around a command post structure, with other buildings nearby.

There was a large Southern Railway depot and carriage works at Lancing, which apart from carrying out repairs and modifications to rolling stock, was also involved in the manufacture of war materials. The 25th Sussex (2nd Southern Railway) Battalion of the Home Guard was formed from its employees in 1940, and later they also manned a troop of Bofors anti-aircraft guns at the Lancing Carriage Works. The Carriage Works was subjected to two bombing raids during the war, the first was on 23 April 1941 and the second more devastating raid was on 30 September 1942, when there was a substantial amount of damage to buildings and rolling stock, but no serious casualties.

Lancing College was taken over by the Army after the pupils and staff had been evacuated in June 1940. A few months later the Army moved out and the College buildings were taken over by the Admiralty as part of HMS King Alfred (see Site 10) until they were handed back in 1945.

The sites today

Two pillboxes survive on this short stretch of coast. The first appears to be a Type 26 variant that has been built into a bank at the top of the beach (TQ 1779 0349) at the west end of Lancing Beach (*colour plate 6*). It has an embrasure (bricked up) facing south across the beach and a small entrance (also now blocked) on its west side where it is approached by a path from the bungalow above. This entrance may be a more recent addition, and there may be other embrasures and an original entrance, but these are hidden by the adjacent garden walls. The outer surface of the pillbox has been rendered, so that it matches the adjacent walls, but this again may be a more recent addition. There is a layer of shingle over the roof in an attempt to camouflage it.

The second pillbox is an unusual type, and probably more correctly called a machine gun emplacement, set low into the sea wall at TQ 2006 0413 towards the east end of Lancing Beach (*20*). Constructed from wood-shuttered concrete, it has a single embrasure in its south-east corner, which suggests that it was intended to cover the beach to its east, enabling it to enfilade the sea wall. Its entrance is in the west wall and on the north side of the sea wall, thereby ensuring that it could be entered under cover. The pillbox has been filled with shingle and therefore access to the interior is impossible. The fact the pillbox is incorporated into the sea wall would suggest that this wall may have been built at the same time as an anti-tank wall to prevent vehicles leaving the beach.

At the west end of Lancing Beach, hundreds of anti-tank cubes were gathered together at the end of the war and buried under Beach Green. Some cubes can be seen eroding out of the earthen bank near the public toilets at TQ 1807 0364, whilst a single cube survives near the car park at TQ 1827 0373. In dry summers numerous parch marks show the location of other buried cubes in the grass

20 An unusual machine gun emplacement built into the sea wall at Lancing Beach (TQ 2006 0413)

between the car park and the beach. The HAA battery to the north of the A259 was removed after the war and the area is now a caravan park (TQ 1985 0455), however, some of the concrete roads probably originate from the battery.

At Lancing recreation ground there are two covered trench air-raid shelters. They are located in the north-east (TQ 1825 0493) and north-west (TQ 1810 0493) corners and show as rectangular mounds. Both have a concrete blast wall at the north end, possibly indicating the original entrance, and the square concrete block on the top may be a blocked emergency exit. There is also a surface air-raid shelter adjacent to Lancing Methodist Church (TQ 1822 0414). It has been converted to public toilets, but the bricked-up entrances in its north wall and its thick concrete roof can be clearly seen. Another surface air-raid shelter survives at Sompting, adjacent to the Community Centre (TQ 1655 0510), which used to be a school. This shelter has a single entrance approached through a gap in the school perimeter wall and is unusual in that it has a double-thickness concrete roof with a number of metal loops along its edge.

The Lancing Carriage Works closed down after the war, but their war memorial for employees killed on active service is now located adjacent to the Lancing war memorial in South Street.

Directions and access

To find the first pillbox, park at the pay and display car park at Beach Green (South Lancing) off the A259. Note the anti-tank cube adjacent to the car park. Walk west across the green, past the public toilets where other anti-tank cubes can be seen projecting from the grassed bank. Walk onto the beach and after 50m the pillbox (which is on private property) can be seen at the top of the beach incorporated into garden walls.

To find the second pillbox, take the road to Shoreham Beach from the roundabout on the A259, turn immediately right into Kings Crescent, follow this to the end and turn right into West Beach Road. Continue along here until you reach the small car park. Continue walking west along Lancing Beach; the pillbox is built into the sea wall behind the beach huts after about 100m.

The air-raid shelters are in the corners of the recreation ground in Crabtree Lane, which is off the A2025 between the A27 and the railway line in Lancing. The surface air-raid shelter is in Yew Tree Close adjacent to Lancing Methodist Church, off South Street (A2025). To find the Sompting air-raid shelter, follow the B2222 from Lancing to Sompting, and turn into Loose Lane. The Community Centre is on the west side of the road, with the shelter located on the left side of the building, however access is only possible when the main gates are open. The caravan park on the position of the HAA battery can be found at the end of The Broadway off the A259.

References/Background reading

Burgess, P. & Saunders, A. 1994, *Blitz over Sussex 1941-42*, Midhurst, Middleton Press
Crook, P. 1998, *Sussex Home Guard*, Midhurst, Middleton Press

SITE 9: SHOREHAM

Period: **Nineteenth century to Second World War**
Type of Site: **Fort, battery and beach defences**

History

Despite an incident in 1628, when some French ships navigated their way into the harbour and captured a small craft, there were no permanent defences constructed at Shoreham Harbour until the mid nineteenth century. A motte or castle is shown as a mound on the north side of the town at the junction of Mill Lane and Southdown Road, on a map of Shoreham published in 1789. It was apparently placed in a state of defence in 1643 by Parliamentarian troops using cannon that had been brought from Rye, but was not threatened as the Royalist troops were repulsed at Bramber (see Site 20).

A fort (also known as the Kingston Redoubt) was built at Shoreham in 1857 to protect the newly constructed entrance to the harbour. It was built in the shape of a lunette with earthen ramparts and gun platform, and was very similar to the fort at Littlehampton (Site 5). A defensible barrack block was situated at the rear, which provided accommodation for 38 officers and men. There was a dry ditch to the front and sides of the fort, which had a loopholed Carnot wall along its bottom (*21*) that continued around the rear to join the defensible barracks. At the three corners

21 The loopholed Carnot wall in the bottom of the ditch at Shoreham Fort, looking east towards the central caponier

of the wall were brick caponiers that were entered from inside the fort, and were loopholed to allow enfilading fire along the front of the wall (*colour plate 7*); the east and west caponiers were also the fort's latrines. The gun platform was designed to take six smooth-bore 68pdr guns, but these were later replaced with five guns, comprising two 80pdr RMLs and three 64pdr RMLs. At either end of the gun platform was an underground magazine. The fort's garrison was provided by the 1st Sussex Volunteer Artillery, who manned it until 1896 when it was disarmed. The fort was subsequently used as a film studio in the early decades of the twentieth century and during the Second World War part of the fort was utilised by an ECB.

During the First World War little appears to have been done to fortify the harbour. However, towards the end of the war, two large concrete towers were built in Shoreham Harbour. Each tower was 190ft tall with a hexagon-shaped base and three six-sided tiers, each one progressively smaller, above this. A round steel turret topped the structure and provided accommodation for 90 men and a mounting for an anti-aircraft gun. The towers were intended to be part of a chain of towers that were to be placed across the Dover Straits with boom nets hung between them to deter German submarines. The war ended before the towers could be deployed; the first tower was towed out of the harbour in 1920 and was lowered onto the seabed off the Isle of White to become the Nab Tower lighthouse. The second tower was found to be too wide to go through the harbour mouth and had to be demolished in 1923-24.

A large hutted camp was built north of Shoreham as the divisional training camp for the 24th Division, part of Kitchener's Third Army. Initially a tented camp in 1914, it quickly became a large camp with wooden huts and other buildings, extending from Mill Hill to Slonk Hill. Well equipped, the camp included a church, post office, a YMCA and a boxing arena adjacent to the camp quartermaster's stores. After the 24th Division moved to France in 1915 the camp was used to train new recruits.

In 1940 the shantytown at Shoreham Beach was evacuated and the civilian population was moved out with all of the buildings, apart from the Church of the Good Shepherd, which was demolished in 1941 to clear the field of fire. A single line of anti-tank cubes was laid along the top of the beach, meandering around the front of the fort and ending at the harbour entrance. Mines, scaffolding and barbed wire were laid on the beach, and a number of pillboxes were constructed at regular intervals and disguised as innocuous buildings. In 1942 Canadian Engineers constructed a concrete emplacement that was to accommodate two 75mm guns and at that time the beach was defended by the 'A' Company of the Edmonton Regiment in carefully concealed two-man weapon pits, with six MMGs in static positions.

Access ramps from the harbour into the town, which was a Nodal Point, were blocked with hairpin rails, whilst the rail and road bridges over the River Adur near the harbour had blocks installed and were covered by a pair of gun emplacements located on the west bank. Old Shoreham Bridge had hairpin rail blocks at either end, and was also covered by a gun emplacement on the west bank. A HAA battery was located on Mill Hill, with four 3.7in HAA guns positioned in square concrete emplacements, together with a command post, radar and other buildings.

Mill Hill and Slonk Hill were defended localities in 1942, manned by the Edmonton Regiment. 'D' Company was positioned on Mill Hill, which was heavily wired and consisted mainly of carefully camouflaged two-man weapon pits. The Company also had three 2pdr anti-tank guns under command and a platoon of the Saskatoon Light Infantry manning MMGs, together with two MMGs manned by its own personnel.

An ECB equipped with two 6in BL Mk II guns and two 90cm searchlights was set up at Shoreham Fort to cover the harbour entrance. The guns were mounted in concrete emplacements built over the moat and Carnot wall of the fort (although there is some evidence that one of the guns was mounted on the east side of the harbour entrance) and the battery OP was built on top of the No. 2 magazine. The defences were supplemented by a 40mm Bofors gun and five UP rockets, whilst an ex US 75mm field gun and spigot mortar provided local defence. One of the searchlights was mounted in a purpose built tower (*22*), whilst the second may have been mounted on the balcony of an adjacent house. The battery was initially manned by 344 Battery, and then 403 Battery of 553 Coast Regiment.

Aldrington Basin in Shoreham Harbour became a Combined Operations Landing Craft base in 1942 under the name of HMS Lizard and provided training facilities for Royal Navy and Royal Marine landing craft crews. A number of buildings around Grand Avenue were requisitioned for accommodation and offices, whilst the ratings accommodation and maintenance base were located at John Brown's Wharf.

Shoreham Airport and its defences are covered under Site 37.

22 The eastern caponier of Shoreham Fort, with the purpose built Emergency Coastal Battery searchlight post adjacent to the harbour entrance

The sites today

Shoreham Fort had been left to decay after the Second World War and its barrack block was demolished in the 1960s. However, the fort was restored in 1978 and is now a Scheduled Ancient Monument, although it is now once again starting to suffer from neglect. The gun platform, gun positions, ditch, Carnot wall and caponiers were all restored to their original nineteenth-century form, and can all be seen today (TQ 2333 0456). Some of the concrete foundations of the barrack block and parts of the parade ground are also visible. A large tower, used by the coastguard until recently, has been added on top of the No. 2 Magazine, and almost certainly originated as the OP for the ECB (*23*). The remains of the ECB gun positions were removed during the restoration, although part of a concrete structure can be seen in the edge of the moat adjacent to the central caponier. On the east side of the fort is a two-storey brick structure with a concrete roof (TQ 2340 0456). Its large aperture at the front (now bricked up) was for a searchlight (*colour plate 8*) and a wartime photograph shows a sandbagged position with a Lewis gun at ground level in front of the structure. A blocked door at ground

23 Shoreham Fort: The gun platform looking west with No. VI gun emplacement in the foreground, and the Observation Post for the Seccond World War Emergency Coastal Battery (subsequently used by the Coastguard) on top of the No. 2 magazine at the far end

level at the rear provided access to the post, with internal steps to the upper storey. Other buildings connected with the ECB may have been located on the north side of the fort and the spigot base is apparently in the garden of a nearby house.

The rows of hut platforms and the roads of the First World War army camp can be clearly seen on an aerial photograph of 1946, together with the zig-zag outline of practice trenches at Slonk Hill and north of Buckingham Barn. However, housing developments and agricultural activities since the Second World War, together with the cut of the new A27 road, have now removed all trace of this large camp. The Second World War HAA battery on Mill Hill is also now under the same housing developments at TQ 2135 0645.

There is no surviving evidence for the gun emplacements on the west bank (approx. TQ211050) of the River Adur covering the rail and road bridges. The only surviving hairpin rail sockets in the town, which comprised five rows of sockets blocking a concrete slipway at Star Gap (TQ 2149 0499), have now been covered over. At Old Shoreham Bridge there are four hairpin rail sockets and the cut-off base of a concrete cube showing in the old road surface on the east side of the bridge (TQ 2072 0596). On the west side of the bridge is a surviving hairpin rail in situ beside the bridge (TQ 2052 0598). The gun emplacement also survives at TQ 2046 0592 and sits on slightly higher ground in the corner of Shoreham Airfield facing east to cover the bridge (see Site 37).

A landing craft (LCVP) has recently been placed in the centre of a roundabout at Shoreham (TQ 2337 0616) to commemorate HMS Lizard.

Directions and access

Shoreham Fort is situated at the end of Shoreham Beach on a road called Forthaven, where there is a pay and display car park. It is open to the public 24 hours a day, every day of the year, and there is a display board near the car park. The Second World War searchlight post can be found on the east side of the fort near the harbour entrance.

Old Shoreham Bridge is on the A283 from Shoreham to the A27, but due to limited parking is actually best approached from the north-east corner of Shoreham Airfield.

Marlipins Museum is situated at 36 High Street, Shoreham and contains information and displays on the various sites around Shoreham, including the fort and Truleigh Hill radar station (Site 22).

Opening times

Shoreham Fort is open to the public at all times.
Marlipins Museum is open Tuesday-Saturday 2nd May-31st October, and also on Bank Holiday Mondays (May-October): 10.30am-4.30pm. Tel: 01273 462994

References/Background reading

Aldsworth, F.G. 1981, 'A Description of the Mid Nineteenth Century Forts at Littlehampton and Shoreham, West Sussex', *Sussex Archaeological Collections* 119, 181-194

Stacey, C.P. 1942, *Situation of the Canadian Forces in the United Kingdom, Spring 1942: III Position and Role of Canadian Forces*, Canadian Military Headquarters Report No. 72

Stafford, J. undated, 'The Mystery Towers: A Shoreham Enigma', *Marlipins Museum Publication* No. 1, Sussex Archaeological Society.

www.shorehamfort.co.uk

SITE 10: HOVE

Period: **Second World War**
Type of Site: **Seafront defences and training establishment**

History

The esplanade at Hove was lined with anti-tank cubes and barbed wire, together with beach scaffolding and mines on the beach. Pillboxes were also constructed at intervals along the seafront.

Along with its neighbour Brighton, the civil defence precautions for Hove had already been prepared and were put into effect immediately after the declaration of war. Numerous air-raid shelters were hastily constructed in the following weeks. Some used existing structures, such as the basements of shops and public buildings, whilst others, particularly those for local schools, were new covered trench shelters. Air-raid warden posts were also constructed across the town, mostly new buildings, but occasionally existing buildings were utilised.

The Hove Marina complex was requisitioned by the Admiralty in 1939 before it had even been opened to the public. Commissioned as HMS King Alfred, the establishment was responsible for the training of RNVR officers and during the war over 22,000 passed through its doors. The swimming bath was covered over and used as the main instructional hall, while the restaurant and dance hall became the wardroom. Other rooms were converted into offices and classrooms, and the large underground car park was also used for accommodation and a ship-handling simulator. Many other local hotels and houses were used for accommodation.

HMS King Alfred also took over the adjacent RNVR facilities, which included a RNR Battery. The battery had been built originally in 1877 and comprised a wooden structure which housed a number of naval artillery pieces that faced out to sea. These guns were used for training, but it is not known whether they would have been utilised in the event of an invasion. After the war, the battery reverted to the Sussex Division RNVR and was used as their HQ until it moved to Shoreham in 1968.

To the north of Hove, the Downs were used as a training area throughout the Second World War, with a number of firing ranges constructed in the dry valleys between Hove and Pyecombe, whilst near Varncombe Hill there was a tank firing range with a moving target. At Devil's Dyke, there is an unusual structure with links to the First World War. The 'Bomb House' was originally an observatory built before 1914, with a wooden platform that allowed people to view the scenery from this vantage point. The aerial cableway that crossed Devil's Dyke was used for testing the dropping of bombs, and perhaps this building was used to store the bombs, hence its name. However, there is no definite link between the two.

24 The King Alfred Centre in Hove was requisitioned at the outbreak of the Second World War, commissioned as HMS King Alfred and used for training RNVR officers.

The sites today

There is nothing surviving today of the Second World War defences in Hove. The Hove Marina was reopened to the public in 1945, and renamed the King Alfred Leisure Centre (*24*), while the RNR Battery was demolished and the area is now a car park for the Leisure Centre. A concrete step in the south-west corner of the car park may mark the location of the Battery. The King Alfred Leisure Centre itself is due to be demolished and the area redeveloped in the near future.

A below-ground air-raid shelter survives at the rear of 47 Cromwell Road (TQ 2946 0529). This property was a girls' school in the 1930s and was requisitioned by Canadian troops during the Second World War, for whom the shelter was constructed. It has stairs down to the shelter from the garden and from inside the house (now blocked); the shelter is currently used as a store by Bellerbys College.

The Bomb House (*colour plate 9*) stands to the west of the Devil's Dyke Hotel and is a rectangular brick structure with no roof (TQ 2569 1088). On passing through the entrance, there is a small (ticket) booth on the left with a concrete roof, while the main part of the structure has been in-filled with earth. A concrete base is all that remains from the aerial cableway (approx. TQ 258108).

A number of Second World War firing ranges have been identified during archaeological fieldwork in the Pyecombe area. A series of in-filled firing trenches are situated in a dry valley near Cow Down (TQ 2850 1220) and evidence of these showed up in the ploughsoil each year when the field was worked. The butts were located at the west end of the valley, and during a fieldwalking exercise numerous spent and unused 0.303 rounds, 2in mortar fins and fragments of Piat rounds were found here.

Directions and access

The King Alfred Leisure Centre is in Kingsway-on-Hove seafront. It has an adjacent car park, and is open every day. There is no access to the air-raid shelter at Cromwell Road.

Devil's Dyke is located at the end of Devil's Dyke Road north of the Red Hill roundabout on the A27. Park in the car park and walk a short distance to the west of the Devil's Dyke Hotel to find the 'Bomb House'. The aerial cableway base can be found near the footpath at the south end of the hotel's car park.

References/Background reading

Butler, C. 2001, 'A Mesolithic and later prehistoric flintworking site at East and West Hills, Pyecombe, West Sussex', *Sussex Archaeological Collections* 139, 7-25

Martin, R. 1996, *Report on unidentified building near Devil's Dyke, Poynings*, unpublished report

http://www.royalnavyresearcharchive.org.uk/KA/King_Alfred_1.htm

3

INLAND SITES

This chapter covers all of the inland sites in West Sussex, excluding airfields (*25*). Although the main focus is on the Second World War Nodal Points that were established in many of the towns and villages, there are also many other types of site covered. The major towns of Chichester and Arundel both suffered sieges during the English Civil War, whilst a number of other sites were the location of small battles or skirmishes. There are also some unusual and very different types of site, for example the Chain Home radar stations at Poling and Truleigh, the direction-finding towers on Halnaker Hill and the training camps and areas at Storrington and Washington.

This chapter also includes the Second World War Corps Stop Line that followed the line of the River Ouse from Uckfield in East Sussex through into West Sussex and then followed the River Arun to Guildford in Surrey. This line was not as

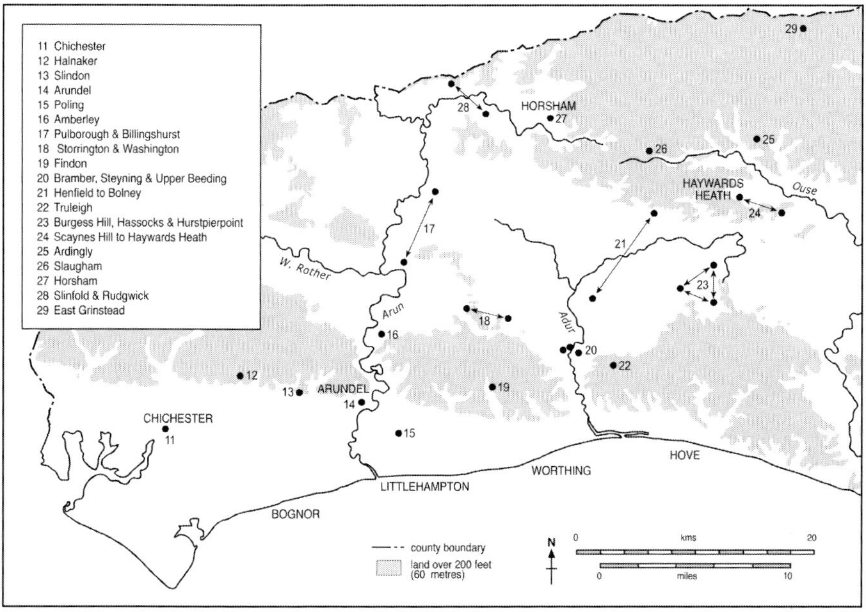

25 Map showing the West Sussex inland sites

strongly defended as the GHQ Stop Line in East Sussex and its pillboxes were concentrated to cover the road bridges over the rivers. There were also other Stop Lines that ran north to south along the Rivers Adur and Arun. The main defensive works on the Stop Lines in West Sussex were the Type 24 pillbox and the Type 28 anti-tank pillbox, along with the open-backed gun emplacements that were unique to the River Adur and River Arun lines, although there were a number of variant pillboxes built to local specifications.

SITE 11: CHICHESTER

Period: **English Civil War to twentieth century**
Type of site: **Barracks and Nodal Point**

History

During the English Civil War, the Royalists took control of Chichester and put the city into a state of defence utilising the Roman city walls. A Parliamentarian army of 6000 men under Sir William Waller arrived before the walls on the 21 December 1642 and besieged the city. Although the walls withstood the bombardment, the attackers managed to bring cannon to within 100 yards of the north gate, and after eight days the garrison surrendered. In 1643 a Royalist army under Sir Ralph Hopton marching to the relief of Arundel Castle was met by Waller's force at West Dean just to the north of Chichester and after a brief skirmish the Royalist force withdrew.

The Chichester Barracks (SU861064) was originally built in 1803 to accommodate 1500 officers and men in timber buildings. It was used continually throughout the nineteenth and twentieth centuries, becoming the Brigade Depot for the Royal Sussex Regiment in 1873. After rebuilds in 1875 and the 1930s, it was renamed Roussillon Barracks in 1958. There was further extensive rebuilding between 1960-64 when it became the training centre for the Royal Military Police, who finally moved out in 2005. The Barracks were the temporary home of Commander Astiz of the Argentine Forces who was a held as a prisoner of war here in 1982.

In 1940 Chichester was established as an anti-tank island and in 1941 the city was designated a Category 'A' Nodal Point. In establishing the defensive perimeter around the city, the defenders (4th Infantry Division) utilised some existing man-made features. Located on the north-west side of the city are a series of discontinuous linear earthworks, called the 'Chichester Entrenchments', which were probably originally created in the Late Iron Age to enclose the Chichester/Selsey area where an *oppidum* (settlement) may have been located. The Entrenchments were modified by placing anti-tank blocks across the earthwork in conjunction with a roadblock that had been positioned on the adjacent Brandy Hole Lane (SU 8545 0664). Another man-made feature utilised was the

Chichester Canal, which formed a suitable anti-tank ditch to the south of the city, although it needed to be refilled as it was little more than a dried-up stream. The canal was modified where necessary to improve its defensive capabilities as an anti-tank ditch; pillboxes and roadblocks defended the road bridges across the canal, whilst the swing bridges were removed. The Upper Lock Keeper's cottage was converted into a strongpoint and slit trenches were dug along the north bank. Hairpin roadblocks blocked entrances into the city, garden walls were loopholed and slit trenches were dug around the north of the city through Lavant. Banks and ditches were dug by hand in the fields around the city to prevent aircraft from landing. The 1st Sussex (Chichester) Home Guard Battalion had an OP on the roof of a water tower at Graylingwell Hospital.

Bofors anti-aircraft guns were positioned in the recreation ground in New Park Road, and smaller anti-aircraft guns were placed on the roofs of Lennards shoe shop at The Cross and on the Gaumont Cinema. The gunners' OP was in the Cathedral tower, although those manning it were not allowed to take their weapons into the Cathedral with them. A 9.2in railway gun was located on a stretch of railway track adjacent to Terminus Road and was later replaced by a 12in railway howitzer.

As with many of the other Sussex towns, public air-raid shelters and ARP wardens' posts were established throughout the city in 1940, with the ARP HQ located in Greyfriars. Twenty-one surface air-raid shelters were built in The Hornet, St Pancras and the four main streets of the city, whilst basements of shops and other properties were also used. The schools were provided with air-raid shelters, including the High School for Boys, where four surface shelters were constructed in the grounds.

A boom was constructed across the mouth of Chichester Harbour in 1940, comprising fixed steel tubular scaffolding across the shallows and a floating boom across the main channel. Chichester Harbour became an important centre during the preparations for the D-Day landings, with landing craft being moored in the channels and the Birdham Pool Shipyard involved in the repair and maintenance of landing craft as part of HMS Sea Serpent. Other shipyards around the harbour were involved in building landing craft, Fairmile MLs and Mulberry harbour sections.

With so many airfields nearby, a large bulk fuel depot was established just before the Second World War on the south-east side of the town, adjacent to the coast railway line. Large underground bunkers were constructed to store the fuel and the depot had its own railway sidings. This site continued to be used into the Cold War period.

The sites today

Although many houses in the suburbs around the town were destroyed or damaged during the short siege in 1642, there was no major damage to the Roman walls or to buildings within the walls. No siege works survive, however the Roman walls can be seen at a number of points around the town.

26 The 'Keep', Rousillon Barracks, Chichester

27 Boundary marker No. 8 at Rousillon Barracks, Chichester

There is nothing remaining of the original Napoleonic barracks apart from some of the flint walls fronting Broyle Road. The large crenellated building near the entrance called the 'Keep' dates from the 1875 rebuilding (*26*); a very similar building can be found at the barracks in Lincoln. This building recently housed the Royal Military Police Museum, although this has now moved out. Within the barracks is a small chapel, which was also originally built in 1875 as a schoolhouse. Most of the other buildings from this period were constructed of wood and have not survived. The remaining barrack buildings at the site all date from the mid twentieth century and are likely to be demolished in the near future to make way for a housing development. Nineteenth-century boundary marker posts can be seen around the barracks, with a gate marker inscribed with '1882' and a War Department boundary marker post at the Wellington Road entrance (SU 8608 0608). Two more boundary marker posts are at the junction of Wellington Road and Broyle Road (*27*), and others can be found along Broyle Road.

There is little surviving evidence for the Second World War defences. The location of the roadblock at Brandy Hole Lane is indicated by the presence of five anti-tank buoys scattered around the bottom of the adjacent Iron Age dyke. These would have originally been placed beside the road so that they could be dragged into place to block it in an emergency. In the bottom of the dyke are five anti-tank cubes (SU 8545 0664) arranged in a zig-zag pattern, corner to corner (*28*), that completely block access along the dyke to vehicles. On the south bank of the dyke there are 25 anti-tank pimples arranged in a pattern of five parallel lines each with five pimples. These pimples would have blocked any vehicle attempting to bypass the roadblock along the south side of the earthwork. Today these pimples stop at the end of the wooded area just beyond the earthwork, and it is not clear whether they would have originally extended any further.

Four surface air-raid shelters survive at Chichester High School for Boys (SU 8632 0423). They have been partly revetted with earth for additional protection and have bricked-up entrances at the south end with an escape hatch in the roof (*colour plate 10*).

South of the town, there are two surviving pillboxes covering bridges across the Chichester Canal. The first is located at Cutfield Bridge on the A286, where a small overgrown pillbox or infantry section post sits on the north bank of the canal (SU 8425 0130). The second pillbox is situated adjacent to the Selsey Tramway drawbridge at SU 8606 0211, although this could not be found in 2007 as there is no public access to the north side of the canal. The tramway had closed in 1935 and the bridge itself was removed during the war.

At Chichester Harbour there are numerous anti-tank cubes incorporated into the seawall of the new marina and along the shore at Salterns Copse (SU829012 to SU829015). Although described as an anti-tank wall in the Defence of Britain database, it is more likely that these have been gathered together from various coastal locations after the war and reused in the sea wall. There are eight anti-tank

28 Five anti-tank cubes block the ditch of the Iron Age earthworks adjacent to Brandy Hole Lane, Chichester (SU 8545 0664)

buoys lining the verge of a minor road at Birdham Pool (SU 8263 0103), with another two nearby.

The shipyard at Birdham (SU 8240 0093) is still operating today. The turntable that was used to haul landing craft up the slipway from the adjacent marina is still in use (*29*), and a number of the original buildings are also present, although two Nissen huts have been removed and the large repair shed was added after the war. The partly sunken wreck of a landing craft can also be seen alongside one of the wooden jetties in Birdham Pool.

The bulk fuel depot is still present (SU 8795 0428), although it is currently lying derelict and may be due for redevelopment. The site comprises four large underground fuel bunkers, together with a number of ancillary buildings and fuel pumps (*30*). A branch line ran from the adjacent railway line to allow for fuel delivery by train.

Directions and access

Roussillon Barracks are located at SU861064 in Broyle Road (A286), Chichester. There is no public access to the barracks, but the 'Keep' can be viewed from Broyle Road. The boundary marker posts can be found in Broyle Road and Wellington Road. The air-raid shelters at the High School for Boys are situated at the edge of the school grounds and can be seen from the adjacent Kingsham Road.

To find the roadblock in the Chichester Entrenchments, take the B2178 (Old Broyle Road) out of Chichester towards Funtington, after crossing the disused railway line turn right into Brandy Hole Lane. Park on the left, then cross the road entering Brandy Hole Copse, walk past the ponds, noting the display panel

29 This turntable at Birdham shipyard was used to haul landing craft up the slipway from the adjacent marina for repairs and is still operating today

30 The bulk fuel depot on the outskirts of Chichester is still extant, although currently lying derelict

situated there, then follow the earthwork for some 200m eastwards until you reach the roadblock.

To find the sites to the south of Chichester, follow the A286 south from the A27. The small pillbox is located on the left just before crossing the Chichester Canal, but is difficult to locate in the undergrowth. Take the minor road to Birdham and turn opposite the church towards Birdham Pool; park near the causeway, from where the shipyard and marina sites can be visited. Return north via the B2145, the Selsey Tramway drawbridge can be seen from the south bank of the canal by following footpaths from Hunston. The bulk fuel depot is situated adjacent to the A27/A259 roundabout, but there is no parking here or access to the site.

References/Background reading

Davenport, C. 2003, 'The Late Pre-Roman Iron Age of the West Sussex Coastal Plain: Continuity or Change', in D. Rudling (ed.) *The Archaeology of Sussex to AD 2000*, Heritage Marketing & Publications Ltd, Kings Lynn

Frampton, D. undated, *The Siege of Chichester 1642*, Academic Artisan Publication

Green, A.H.J. 2005, *The History of Chichester's Canal*, Sussex Industrial Archaeological Society

Grehan, J. 2001, *Battles & Battlefields of Sussex*, Storrington, Historic Military Press

Hewitt, P. 2004, *Chichester Remembered*, Chichester, Phillimore & Co Ltd

Macdougall, P. 2004, *The Story of Chichester*, Stroud, Sutton Publishing Ltd

Morgan, R.R. 1991, 'Chichester's Civil War Scars', *Sussex Archaeological Collections*, 129, 253-255

Price, B. 1978, *Chichester: The Valiant Years*, Chichester, Phillimore & Co Ltd

Reger, J. 1996, *Chichester Harbour – A History*, Chichester, Phillimore & Co Ltd

Smith, M. 2004, *Chichester Harbour – An informed look at the last one hundred years*, Chichester Harbour Conservancy

SITE 12: HALNAKER

Period: **Second World War**
Type of Site: **Direction-Finding Towers and OP**

History

Halnaker Hill to the east of Chichester at 128m above sea level has commanding views south over the coastal plain to the coast. In the Second World War, direction-finding equipment was installed on the hilltop to take advantage of this location.

Four octagonal brick-built structures were constructed on the hilltop, on the south, south-east, east and north sides of the hill. The first three had an

1 Machine gun emplacement (SZ 8319 9462) built into the bank at Broad Rife, Selsey. The entrance and one of the two embrasures can be seen here on the east side of the emplacement

2 This structure is probably the searchlight post for the Right Section of the Bognor Regis ECB. Added onto a pre-war building, the searchlight post stands on stilts and has been converted into a beach house

3 Littlehampton Fort: part of the Carnot wall and an open bastion, now very overgrown

4 The searchlight post at Angmering Emergency Coastal Battery, now used as a beach house

5 The loopholed wall in Brougham Road, Worthing. The loopholes were positioned to cover the approaching road from the seafront, and have now been blocked with a different coloured type of brick

6 Type 26 pillbox at Lancing Beach. Note the blocked embrasure and external rendering

7 The central caponier at Shoreham Fort

8 The searchlight post at the harbour entrance for the Emergency Coastal Battery located at Shoreham Fort

9 The 'Bomb House' at Devils Dyke may have been used to store bombs that were used on the nearby aerial cableway during the First World War

10 Four surface air-raid shelters in the grounds of Chichester High School for Boys

11 Halnaker Hill. One of the radio direction finding towers on the hill, with Halnaker Windmill, which was used as an observation post by the Home Guard, in the background

12 Probable Civil War earthworks on the west side of Arundel Castle

13 Training emplacement on the South Downs at Washington (TQ 1117 1200)

14 The blackout markings on Beeding Bridge

15 Gun emplacement at Coombes (TQ 1951 0875) covering the now dismantled railway bridge across the River Adur

16 Type 28A pillbox at Pilstye Farm (TQ 3075 2831), north of Cuckfield covers the bridge over the River Ouse on the B2036

17 Two of the four anti-tank coffins still in-situ at Slaugham Lane Bridge (TQ 2516 2745)

18 An unusual two-storey pillbox in woodland south of Furnace Pond, Slaugham (TQ 2496 2788)

19 Type 24 pillbox built into a low bank on the edge of High Wood (TQ 1482 2985), near Christ's Hospital, Horsham

20 Type 28 pillbox at Bucks Green (TQ 0843 3274): Note the use of two different types of brick, which was part of its camouflage as a farm building. It also had a tiled roof and clapboard walls.

21 The Control Tower at Tangmere; now derelict and boarded up

22 The Parachute Store at Westhampnett Airfield is currently used as a shop

23 A Blister Hangar survives at Ford Airfield (SU 9949 0236)

24 The unique Gunnery Training Dome at Shoreham Airfield

25 An octagonal-shaped pillbox built into the embankment of the River Adur on the east side of Shoreham Airfield (TQ 2076 0535)

octagonal concrete base with a central holdfast, surrounded by a brick wall 2.6m high, with an entrance on the south-east corner; these were topped by a wooden structure, which contained the radio direction-finding fixer equipment. The direction-finding equipment worked by each of the three towers picking up a signal from an aircraft, the bearings of which were used to fix the position of the aircraft. The fourth octagonal structure was topped with a concrete roof, through which was a small entrance into the interior. Alongside this structure was a large metal tank, with pipe-work running from it into the brick structure. There were also a number of ancillary buildings on the hilltop.

Halnaker windmill is a tile-hung brick tower mill, built in 1750 for Goodwood Estates, and had been derelict until it was restored in 1934. During the Second World War the windmill was used as an OP by the Home Guard.

The sites today

The wooden structures that topped the three octagonal direction-finding fixer towers have long since gone, but the lower brickwork and concrete bases survive to varying degrees. One tower (No. 3), on the south-east side of the hill (SU 9207 0964) and constructed from red bricks, is almost complete, although a little overgrown (*colour plate 11*). On the east side a second tower (No. 2) is constructed from soft white bricks (SU 9211 0973) and has been partly demolished. The third tower (No. 4) is on the south side (SU 9196 0961) and has been demolished to ground level with only the concrete base and holdfast surviving. This tower was also constructed from white bricks and has an adjacent rectangular concrete base on its west side, presumably for a building. A similar concrete base (or perhaps the roof of a buried structure) is situated on the east side of the hill (SU 9210 0971). The fourth octagonal structure (No. 1) is located on the north side of the hill (SU 9205 0982), with its large metal tank alongside (*31*). There is a single pipe that runs from the north end of the tank via a pump mechanism and valves before emerging inside the structure. The interior walls are covered with soot and the only access is through a square hole in the roof. It has been suggested that this structure was for creating a smokescreen, although it is more likely that it was the engine room providing power for the co-located direction-finders.

The windmill is currently disused, although it has been recently renovated, and is an empty shell with only beams for the upper floors and the cap is floorboarded (SU 9199 0964). There is no evidence for any modifications associated with its wartime use as an OP.

Directions and access

Park in a layby on the A285 near Seabeach House, or at the bottom of Mill Lane, and follow the footpaths to Halnaker Hill. On approaching the gate, Tower 4 is in a field on your left, but should not be approached if there is a crop in the field. Go

31 Halnaker Hill: This brick-built octagonal structure has its entrance in the roof and a large metal tank alongside it, with pipe-work connecting the two. It may have been the engine room for the adjacent direction-finding towers

through the gate, the windmill is directly in front of you, and Tower 3 is a short distance on the right. Continue past Tower 3 to find Tower 2 and the concrete base, and then a little further north is Tower 1 and its associated tank.

References/Background reading

Mace, M.F. 1997, *Sussex Wartime Relics and Memorials*, Storrington, Historic Military Press

Martin, R.G. 1996, *Radio Direction Tower Bases, Halnaker Hill* (unpublished drawing)

Oswald, A. & Dyer, C. 1995, *Halnaker Hill, Chichester, West Sussex,* Archaeological Field Survey Report, Cambridge, RCHME

www.sussexmillsgroup.org.uk

SITE 13: SLINDON

Period: **First and Second World Wars**
Type of Site: **Airship mooring-out station and decoy site**

History

In April 1918 a mooring-out station for airships was established at Slindon as part of the RNAS airship base at Polegate in East Sussex. Up to two SSZ airships were based at the Slindon mooring-out station, which was located in a sheltered valley near Northwood Cottages (SU 9585 1000), and was considered to be one of the best mooring-out sites in the group. The site was abandoned shortly after the Armistice.

In April 1940 a 'K' decoy site (No. 51a) was set up at Gumber Farm as a daylight decoy for RAF Tangmere, which is located some 8km to the south-west. The site was equipped with dummy Hurricanes manufactured by Green Brothers in Hailsham. Later in 1940 the site was modified to also become a 'Q' decoy site to simulate night operations at Tangmere. A partly sunken shelter was built to control the lighting, with an air-raid shelter nearby. The personnel were billeted at Gumber Farm, along with two farm worker families and Land Army girls. The site does not appear to have been very successful, as a German aerial photograph has subsequently been discovered with the site marked as a dummy airfield!

The sites today

There is no surviving evidence for the airship mooring-out station, however, as the only fixed installations were concrete mooring posts, it may be that these remain to be discovered, or were removed after the war.

The fixed installations for the Q decoy site survive remarkably well at Gumber Farm, although there is no evidence for the actual lighting and decoy site itself. The control shelter is located just to the north of Gumber Farm (SU 9609 1199) and conforms to the standard shelter specified for these decoy sites. It has been partly buried with earth for additional protection, and although in good condition, it has become the home for a family of badgers. The shelter comprises an entrance protected by blast walls, with a control room on the left and a generator room on the right (*32*). The control room resembles a small Nissen hut and has an emergency exit, again protected by blast walls, at the south end. The generator room is built from prefabricated concrete sections resembling a small Stanton shelter and has an exhaust outlet pipe on the north side. Outside on the north side is a small box manufactured from concrete sections, which may be the headlamp, and was supposed to simulate a taxiing aircraft.

Located 50m south of the control shelter is a small covered air-raid shelter (SU 9610 1191). This is accessed by stairs at the west end and has been constructed from prefabricated concrete panels, with an escape hatch in the roof at the east end.

At Gumber Farm the cottages in which the personnel were accommodated, alongside the Land Army girls and farm workers, are still standing. There is a small brick-built air-raid shelter with a concrete roof situated in the garden of the cottages (SU 9622 1188).

The exact location of the dummy lighting layout is not clear and in 1940 the slope to the north of Gumber Farm was scrub. It is possible that the line of the

32 The control shelter for the Q decoy site at Gumber Farm, Slindon (SU 9609 1199). The main entrance is on the right, whilst the emergency exit from the control room is on the left. The fallen pieces of concrete appear to have been part of an external blast wall

Roman road Stane Street, which shows as a distinct earthwork to the north-west, was used.

Directions and access

From Slindon village, walk up the minor road through Courthill Farm, follow this to where the footpaths diverge near Northwood Cottages and take the right fork. The airship mooring-out station was located in the field on your left between the wood and the cottages. Carry on along the footpath, past Warren Barn to Gumber Farm, and then continue through the farm; the control shelter and air-raid shelter are situated behind the lambing shelters on the left.

The sites at Slindon are all on National Trust land, but whilst there is access via the footpaths, the actual sites are on tenanted farmland and should not be approached from the footpath when animals are in the field. There is no access to the interior of the shelters.

National Trust Slindon Estate Office Tel. 01243 814730

References/Background reading

Ashworth, R.C.B. 1985, *Action Stations 9. Military airfields of the Central South and South-East*, Wellingborough, Patrick Stephens Ltd

Dobinson, C. 2000, *Fields of Deception*, London, Methuen Publishing Ltd

SITE 14: ARUNDEL

Period: **English Civil War to Second World War**
Type of Site: **Castle and Nodal Point**

History

Arundel Castle was regarded as being the most powerful castle in the country at the start of the sixteenth century, but when the Parliamentarian army sent a small force to capture it in December 1642, its garrison of 100 men quickly surrendered after the main gate was blown in. In December 1643, a Royalist force led by Sir Ralph Hopton arrived at Arundel and after capturing the town, laid siege to the castle, which quickly surrendered. A Parliamentarian army of around 6000 men under General Waller then marched on Arundel to find the garrison of over 1000 men had thrown up new earthworks around the town and castle. After a preliminary artillery bombardment, the earthworks on the north and south-west sides of the town were captured, and despite a sortie from the castle, the town was also taken. Two light artillery pieces were lifted up to the tower of Arundel church and, together with the musketeers, began to fire onto the castle battlements. The Parliamentarian army was reinforced, and in an effort to deny the garrison its water supply, they drained Swanbourne Lake. A relief force under Hopton failed to make any progress after a skirmish at West Dean, north of Chichester, and with reduced water and food rations, and under bombardment from Parliamentary cannons, the Royalist garrison finally surrendered on 6 January 1644. The castle was slighted in 1649 and left roofless and ruined.

Arundel was designated a Category 'A' Nodal Point during the Second World War. Roadblocks were placed on the roads into the town, and were covered by pillboxes built by 262 Field Company RE and local contractors, including one at The Slipe and others built in back gardens facing south and south-east. A Type 28 pillbox, covering the roadblock at Arundel Bridge, was built up against the south-east gate of the castle and was camouflaged using flint to blend in with the castle walls. A number of infantry section posts lined the bank on the west side of Mill Road, facing the river, whilst at least one more infantry section post was located on the north side of the Castle Park. The posts along Mill Lane were open-backed with loopholed front and side walls built of brick and concrete, and a wooden roof supported by a steel girder. Some houses in the town were fortified by the addition of blast walls and reinforced floors, and a *flame fougasse* was built in the Causeway. Artillery was positioned in Arundel Park, which provided a vantage point overlooking the coastal plain down to the coast at Littlehampton. Further gun emplacements were located north of the town, covering bridges that crossed the River Arun.

In June 1940, the east wing of the castle was taken over by the army and was used by British (including 7th Guards Brigade), Canadian and American troops until 1945. The Home Guard manned an OP at night on the South Tower, whilst the Observer Corps used the roof of St Martin's Chapel in the Keep of the castle as an OP. The town escaped any direct air attacks and there were no civilian deaths as a result of German bombing during the war. A number of air-raid shelters were built in the town and civil defence preparations were made.

The sites today

The castle as seen today is largely the result of rebuilding in the nineteenth and twentieth centuries and there is little evidence of the damage inflicted during the sieges of the Civil War. A V-shaped earthwork on the north-west side of the castle covering the London road (TQ 0131 0744) may be one of the earthworks raised by the Royalist garrison in 1643 and was possibly adapted from an earlier outer work of the castle (*colour plate 12*). Damage in the Fitzalan Chapel was caused by Waller's Parliamentarian troops who used it as a stable for their horses. An earthwork along the Burpham Road at TQ 0302 0683 may have been an artillery position for the Parliamentarian cannon.

The infantry section posts along Mill Lane (*33*) were demolished in the 1980s, but one survives to the north of Castle Park at TQ 0162 0782. It comprises a sunken narrow rectangular brick structure with three embrasures along its main wall facing north and smaller embrasures in each end wall. The entrance has been partly demolished, but may have originally formed an L-shape, with steps down into the interior. The roof has been removed, leaving a steel girder support exposed.

Although there is nothing remaining of the Observer Corps post on the roof of St Martin's Chapel in the Castle Keep (*34*), there are a number of telephone cable wire clips still in situ on the external wall of the Chapel. The castle was used by British and Canadian troops for accommodation, some of whom carved their names and numbers on the Bevis Tower. Incidentally, troops waiting to board their landing ships for D-Day were parked along Mill Lane in 1944 and many carved their names on the trees.

The surviving evidence for the roadblock at Arundel Bridge, comprises a single anti-tank hairpin rail socket in the pavement on the west side of the bridge (TQ 0195 0702) with a second filled-in socket at the edge of the pavement. A roadblock was positioned at the south end of Maltravers Street, with two loopholes in the flint wall of the Arundel Free School (now the library) covering it (TQ 0145 0694). Two further loopholes are in a flint wall at the east end of the school at the junction of Surrey Street and School Lane; all of them have now been blocked. A pillbox was apparently positioned in the field to the west of Maltravers Street (approx. TQ 0140 0695), but has been demolished since the war. Arundel Free School also had five air-raid shelters in its playground, some of which were located to the right of the entrance and others on the east side against the flint wall adjacent to Maltravers Street, where some brickwork bonded into the flint wall may mark their location.

33 One of the Infantry section posts along Mill Lane that survived until the 1980s. *Photograph: Eric Nash*

34 Arundel Castle Keep: The Observer Corps used the roof of St Martin's Chapel, which is the square structure on the left side of the Keep

At Offham north of Arundel, a single gun emplacement is located in woodland (TQ 0268 0857) on the high ground facing north-east across a field to cover a small farm bridge across the River Arun. The bridge itself had a roadblock of

35 Anti-tank hairpin rail sockets Offham Bridge to the north of Arundel

anti-tank hairpin rails, for which there is surviving evidence in the form of a row of three sockets and a second row of two sockets set into concrete on the west side of the bridge (*35*). Similar concrete on the east side of the bridge may be evidence of further sockets or perhaps anti-tank cubes between the bridge and the railway line.

On the A284 between Arundel and Bury there are two anti-tank buoys on the verge at the entrance to Green Doors Lodge (TQ 0070 0822).

Directions and access

To visit Arundel Castle, park in the large (pay and display) car park opposite the entrance in Mill Road, or in Mill Road itself. The Keep can be visited, but Bevis Tower and other parts of the castle are not open to the public. The surviving infantry section post can be seen in woodland from the open ground to the north of Castle Park (the cricket ground), although it is very overgrown and there is no direct access to it. Arundel Bridge is in the centre of the town, close to the castle entrance. Parking is very limited near Maltravers Street, so it is best to walk there; the two loopholes can be seen in the section of flint walling at its junction with Surrey Street.

The Civil War siege battery position can be found by taking the Burpham road from the A27 opposite Arundel railway station. Follow this for 600m and you will find it on the right side of the road.

The gun emplacement at Offham is located on the high ground above the Black Rabbit public house, but is difficult to find. Drive north along Mill Road and park near the Black Rabbit. Walk past the pub until you get to a stile, then head upslope and follow one of the numerous paths through the wood to find the gun emplacement. Go back to the stile and continue walking north-east along the side of the river until you reach the small bridge, where you will find the hairpin rail sockets.

Opening times
Arundel Castle is open from spring to autumn; Tuesday to Sundays inclusive, and August Mondays and Bank Holiday Mondays. Tel: 1903 882173

References/Background reading

Curwen, E.C. 1930, *Sussex from the Air*, Arundel, Sussex County Magazine

Freeman, W. undated, *Arundel Castle: History and Guide Book*, 20th edition, Brighton, The Southern Publishing Company Ltd

Grehan, J. 2001, *Battles & Battlefields of Sussex*, Storrington, Historic Military Press

Guy, N. (ed.) 2005/6, 'Arundel Castle', *The Castle Studies Group Journal* No. 19, 9-24

Hagedorn, R., Umbima, P., Lishman, V. & English, A. (eds) 2000, *Arundel Voices*, Arundel, Arundel Museum Society

Mace, M.F. 1996, *Frontline Sussex: The Defence Lines of West Sussex 1939-1945*, Storrington, Historic Military Press

Preston, J.H. 1993, *Arundel*, London, Associated University Press

SITE 15: POLING

Period: **Second World War**
Type of Site: **Radar Station**

History

The Chain Home and Chain Home Low radar station at RAF Poling was still under construction at the start of the Second World War, but was operational during the Battle of Britain. There were four transmitter towers in a line on the western part of the site with curtain arrays slung between them (one tower was removed later) and a transmitter block. Four receiver towers were positioned at the corners of a square on the eastern part of the site with a receiver block at their centre. Around these structures were a number of administrative buildings, a pair of Air Ministry houses and air-raid shelters. The buried reserves were located further south near Poling village. A number of pillboxes were also built around RAF Poling to provide local protection in the event of a ground attack and some Bofors anti-aircraft guns were located nearby for air defence.

RAF Poling, along with the airfields at Ford and Thorney Island, was heavily attacked by the Luftwaffe on the 18 August 1940. Thirty-one Stuka dive bombers of IIIrd Gruppe, Geschwader 77, struck in the early afternoon and, despite the defensive fire from Bofors, caused damage to one of the wooden receiver towers, which put the Chain Home set out of action for a week, although the Chain Home Low set remained operational.

The radar station continued in operation throughout the rest of the war and for a number of years afterwards, and was only stood down in 1955, with the masts being removed a few years later.

The site today

With the masts gone, much of the site was demolished, but there remain a number of components of the radar station to be seen today. The receiver block (TQ 0449 0511), albeit with its external blast wall removed, was used for many years as a garage and workshop, but has now been converted into a house (*36*). The walls have been raised in height and a pitched roof added, but there are still telltale bomb splinter scars on the original brickwork. The Air Ministry houses (TQ 0439 0508) are now private dwellings and also have concrete filled bomb splinter scars in their brickwork. On the northern perimeter of the site stands a water tower (approx. TQ 0433 0517) and the original concrete road leading the to Air Ministry houses is still in use today.

The local defences were mostly removed after the war and only a single pillbox now remains. This is recorded as being a Type 22 pillbox, with an external blast wall protecting its entrance, but it was too overgrown when visited recently to be certain of its type (TQ 0409 0469). It faces south to cover a track that approaches the radar station from Littlehampton. In Poling village there are two anti-tank buoys on the side of the road at TQ 0465 0487.

36 The receiver block, albeit without its surrounding blast wall, survives at the site of Poling radar station and has now been converted into a house

Directions and access

Turn off the A27 to Poling village; the receiver block and Air Ministry houses are along the original concrete road (signposted 'Radar Barn') to the radar station, although this is now private property. Continue to Poling village, past a possible bomb crater on the right side of the road and past the anti-tank buoys on the sharp left-hand corner, to park outside the church. From here, walk west along Poling Street and then follow the footpath for a further 200m until you reach a junction, turn left to find the pillbox hidden in the hedge on the right of the track. A plaque in the church provides a little background information and some photographs of the radar station.

References/Background reading

Mace, M.F. 1997, *Sussex Wartime Relics and Memorials*, Storrington, Historic Military Press

Price, A. 1990, *The Hardest Day: The Battle of Britain 18 August 1940*, London, Arrow Books Ltd

SITE 16: AMBERLEY

Period: **English Civil War to Second World War**
Type of Site: **Castle & Nodal Point**

History

Amberley Castle began life as a hunting lodge built by Bishop Luffa in 1103. It was enlarged and developed over time, and permission was given to crenellate in 1377. During the English Civil War, Amberley Castle was occupied by the Royalist John Goring, who encouraged the local population to resist Parliament's demand for money to fund the war. General Waller marched the five miles from Arundel in January 1644 and seized Amberley Castle, although there is no evidence of a siege or damage from bombardment. The Castle was slighted and many of the internal buildings destroyed, it was then sold by the Parliamentary Commissioners in 1648.

The important road bridge (now on the B2139) crossing the River Arun at Amberley Bridge (TQ 0250 1183) was designated a Category 'A' Nodal Point in 1940, although very little is known about the defences covering the bridge. Gun emplacements were constructed to cover the bridges to the south and north of Amberley. A roadblock, including curved rails (hairpins) in sockets, was placed to block the small farm bridge at South Stoke and was covered by a gun emplacement located at South Stoke Farm, to the south-west of the bridge. Timberley Bridge which carried the railway line over the River Arun north of Amberley was covered by two gun emplacements, one on each side of the river.

A Home Guard training school was established at the disused chalk pits at Amberley in 1941. The school ran a range of different courses for officers and men under the guidance of regular army instructors, and later from Canadian troops. There does not appear to have been much in the way of infrastructure at the Amberley training school beyond a number of Nissen huts.

The sites today

Amberley Castle (TQ 0270 1310) is now run as a hotel and restaurant, and there is little to see of the castle itself from the outside. Two anti-tank pimples apparently block a track to the south of Church Street in Amberley (approx. TQ028132), but could not be located in 2007, although they may be on a private track that runs south beside the church. One of the gun emplacements covering Timberley Bridge can be found just to the west of the castle and is now incorporated into a private garden. It is situated on a low bluff overlooking a track (TQ 0249 1318) and faces north towards the bridge. The other gun emplacement is situated on the west side of the river near Timberley Cottages (TQ 0188 1410). It faces south to cover the bridge and has been altered since the war for use as a garage.

At South Stoke there is no trace of the sockets for the hairpin rails (located approx. TQ026102) in the road leading to the bridge, the bridge itself has recently been replaced and the road re-surfaced, so all trace of the roadblock has presumably been erased. The adjacent gun emplacement is located on the higher ground at South Stoke Farm (TQ 0259 1004) and faces towards the bridge (*37*). It is hidden behind a garden wall, which apparently predates the emplacement; presumably the intention was that a section of the wall would be demolished in the event of an invasion. It is possible that there was another emplacement on the north side of the river, but no trace of this survives today. There is also no trace of any surviving defences at Amberley Bridge.

The chalk pits at Amberley are now open to the public as a working museum and it is possible to find a number of trenches on the woodland trail (TQ028122) that may date from its use as a Home Guard training school.

Directions and access

Amberley Castle is located on the west side of Amberley Village, with a separate access for guests from the B2139. Parts of the outer walls can be seen from the west end of Church Street. To find the gun emplacement at Amberley continue along the footpath at the end of Church Street, the emplacement is located on the bluff on the left above the footpath, just before you reach the railway line. The second gun emplacement is along a private road to Timberley Farm from the A29. The bridge at South Stoke can be reached by taking Mill Road from Arundel, then following the minor road through Offham to South Stoke. There is very limited parking here and no access to the gun emplacement, although it can be seen from the footpath which runs through the farm. The entrance to Amberley Working Museum is adjacent to Amberley railway station on the B2139.

37 The Gun emplacement positioned behind a farm wall at South Stoke (TQ 0259 1004)

Opening times

Amberley Castle is not open for public visits, but reservations for the hotel and restaurant can be made. Tel. 01798 831992

Amberley Working Museum is open Wednesday to Sunday and Bank Holiday Mondays between mid March and late October. Tel. 01798 831370

References/Background reading

Crook, P. 1998, *Sussex Home Guard*, Midhurst, Middleton Press

Grehan, J. 2001, *Battles & Battlefields of Sussex*, Storrington, Historic Military Press

www.amberleycastle.co.uk

SITE 17: PULBOROUGH AND BILLINGSHURST

Period: **Second World War**
Type of Site: **Nodal Points**

History

Pulborough was in an important location with its road and rail bridges across the River Arun and was therefore designated a Nodal Point. Barbed wire was laid along the north bank of the river and fields on both side of the river were covered with anti-landing posts and wire. A hairpin rail roadblock was established at Swan Corner across three intersecting roads and strongpoints were established on the west side of the Masonic Hall and on Church Hill. Three gun emplacements were built on the high ground north of the river; one beside the churchyard, one in the corner of Castle Field and the third above the White Hart. A fourth was built on the other side of the river near Winters Farm, but was demolished a few weeks later as it had been incorrectly sited. The Home Guard had their HQ in the Swan Hotel.

The ARP had their HQ in Allfrey's yard in Lower Street and the Firewatchers posts were on the roof of the Arun Hotel and in the church tower. There were only two air-raid shelters in the village, the first was at St Mary's School and the second was in the yard of Harwoods Garage in London Road. There was also an Observer Corps post in the village, located in the area of Glebelands to the rear of Alpha Cottages.

Billingshurst, some 6km further north, was also a Nodal Point covering the important crossroads of the A29 and A272. At Coldwaltham, 3km south of Pulborough, there were two gun emplacements covering Greatham Bridge across the River Arun. Wiggonholt Common, south-east of Pulborough, was used as a training area by Canadian soldiers based at Parham House.

The sites today

Two of the gun emplacements on the hill above the River Arun survive today. The first is situated in a small field alongside the churchyard (TQ 0463 1873) and

38 Gun emplacement in the corner of Castle Field, Pulborough (TQ 0396 1891), which faces south-east to cover the railway bridge

faces south to cover Pulborough Bridge. The second is situated in the corner of Castle Field (TQ 0396 1891) and faces south-east to cover the railway bridge (*38*). Both of these are standard concrete gun emplacements with a large embrasure at the front and a broad open rear face to take a wheeled field gun. A pillbox on the north-west side of Pulborough Bridge (at approx. TQ045186) could not be found and has almost certainly been removed to make way for recent waterfront developments here. A single anti-tank hairpin rail socket survives from the roadblock in the pavement at Swan Corner (TQ 0464 1858).

At Greatham Bridge both of the gun emplacements survive. The first is on the west side of the river and is located at the edge of a field (TQ 0260 1615) facing north-east to cover the bridge. The second is hidden amongst the buildings at Quell Farm (approx. TQ 0335 1590) on the east side of the river and faces north-west. At Wiggonholt Common there are some partly in-filled training trenches amongst the trees (TQ 0609 1628), most of which have been planted since the war.

The only evidence for the Nodal Point at Billingshurst are four anti-tank pimples sitting in the front gardens of 99 and 101 High Street (TQ 0863 2576) which must indicate the former presence of a roadblock at this location (*39*). Around Billingshurst there are numerous anti-tank buoys positioned at the entrances to farms and other properties, including five at Hunger Hill (TQ 1150 2058), four at South Goringlee (TQ 1011 2085), two at Wharf Farm (TQ 0667 2597) and two at Streele Farm (TQ 0724 2500), all of which probably originated from roadblocks nearby.

39 Two of the anti-tank pimples in the front gardens of 101 High Street, Billingshurst, indicating the former presence of a roadblock at this location

Directions and access

The gun emplacements in Pulborough are along Church Place, which is a narrow lane with limited parking. The first is located in a private field at the rear of the church and is best seen from the south-west corner of the churchyard. Continue on across the railway line, past Old Place and into Coombelands Lane. Take a footpath on the left around the edge of a field towards Park Mound; the gun emplacement is situated at the edge of the field.

Swan Corner is at the junction of the A29 and A283, there is limited parking here. The hairpin rail socket is in the pavement between the two mini roundabouts. For Coldwaltham, follow the A29 south and turn left towards Greatham Bridge. The first gun emplacement can be seen on the left beyond some farm buildings a short distance after crossing the railway; the second is almost impossible to see at Quell Farm. The trenches at Wiggonholt Common are best reached from the car park at the Pulborough Brooks RSPB reserve.

The anti-tank pimples in Billingshurst can be found at the south end of the High Street, just before the junction with West Street (A272) and opposite a small church. There are two pimples in each garden, although they are becoming overgrown.

References/Background reading

Morris D.W. 1995, *Pulborough in War Time 1939-1945*, private publication

SITE 18: STORRINGTON AND WASHINGTON

Period: **Second World War**
Type of Site: **Training areas and camps**

History

The South Downs at Storrington and Washington were taken over as training areas from early in the war, although initially the focus was on defence in the event of a German invasion. Washington, sitting astride the A24 from Worthing to London, became a Category 'A' Nodal Point, and Chanctonbury Ring was turned into a defended locality. The defended locality was prepared for all-round defence with a wired perimeter and fire positions, and it was manned by a single infantry company with four MMGs and two 2pdr anti-tank guns in support. The HQ for the Emergency Coastal Batteries between Bognor and Brighton was located at Washington, probably in the Old Vicarage.

With the build-up of Allied forces during the lead-up to D-Day, numerous training camps were constructed at the foot of the Downs to house the troops and to allow easy access onto the Downland training areas. Three camps called East Park Wall, Windmill Hill and Strawberry Grove were built by Canadian Engineers in the grounds of the Parham Estate, west of Storrington, in 1942, with the 2nd

Canadian Division based at Parham House. These troops also used Wiggonholt Common for training (see Site 17). Barns Farm Camp at Sullington had been built earlier in the war to house British and Canadian troops and later became a Royal Signals training establishment. After the war, Barns Farm Camp was used by National Servicemen before it was decommissioned in the later 1950s.

A tank road was constructed by widening and metalling an existing farm track from the B2139 up onto the Downs at Springhead Hill to enable tanks to climb the steep slope. Two firing ranges were built side by side by Canadian Engineers in 1942/3 on the site of an earlier range from the Napoleonic Wars at Kithurst Farm, Storrington. The ranges continued to be used after the war and only closed in the 1980s.

Windlesham House at Washington became the Royal Canadian School of Infantry in 1942 and also housed the HQ of the Department of Petroleum Warfare. Canadian Engineers built a number of unusual concrete emplacements on the Downs nearby, perhaps for testing flame-throwers, although their exact purpose is unclear.

The sites today

At Storrington the tank road runs from the B2139 at TQ 0655 1333 to Springhead Hill (TQ 0706 1247). One of the concrete training emplacements is situated in a small copse south of Kithurst Hill (TQ 0744 1180). It is almost unrecognisable today, showing up as lumps of concrete hidden amongst the bushes and mixed up with other military debris, having been partly demolished or perhaps destroyed by shelling or explosives.

The hulk of a Churchill Mk II tank, a remarkable remnant of the training that was taking place here during the war, survives at the edge of a field south of Springhead Hill (TQ 0722 1207). The Churchill tank belonged to the 'A' Squadron of the 14th Canadian Army Tank Regiment (The Calgary Regiment) and had suffered a serious mechanical failure in 1942. It was stripped of its engine and armament, and was then used for target practice throughout the rest of the war. At the end of the war it was tipped into a nearby bomb crater, where it remained until it was rediscovered and recovered in 1993.

There is no access to Kithurst Range, which is situated on private farmland beside the B2139 (TQ 0730 1335), although the concrete road leading to the range can be seen. The surviving Nissen huts at Strawberry Grove Camp at Parham (TQ 0625 1520) are now part of a sawmill and are not accessible to the public. Barns Farm Camp at Storrington is now largely demolished and partly redeveloped (TQ 1060 1320). The perimeter fence is still present and the large REME workshops and garage is currently used as a warehouse. Most of the other buildings have been demolished, but a single wooden hut and a Nissen hut, together with numerous concrete hut bases, can still be seen. Nearby are nine anti-tank cylinders built into an earthen bank at the entrance to a disused sandpit (TQ 1091 1366), with perhaps others hidden within the bank.

40 Training emplacement on the South Downs at Washington (TQ 1117 1200). This photo shows its method of construction from concrete blocks with an outer covering of metal plates, and sandwiched between the two is a layer of concrete and pitch

At Washington, three of the concrete training emplacements survive on the Downs to the west of the A24. The first is at Highden Beaches (TQ 1107 1142), within the grounds of Windlesham House, and cannot be visited. It is of an unusual design and constructed from corrugated iron-shuttered concrete, with a similarly constructed roof. The second emplacement is the best preserved (*colour plate 13*) and is situated on Highden Hill (TQ 1117 1200). It is a large seven-sided structure of a unique design; constructed from concrete blocks with an outer covering of metal plates and a layer of concrete and pitch sandwiched between the two (*40*). There is a small entrance on the east side with an internal blast wall, both this and the main wall are internally strengthened with buttresses at regular intervals. There are three small embrasures with internal concrete tables, although these have very limited fields of fire confirming that it never had a defensive role. A similar emplacement is located a little further west (TQ1057 1185). This appears to have been constructed in the same way as the previous emplacement, but its roof has collapsed and much of the external cladding has fallen away.

Chanctonbury Ring (TQ139121) is a hillfort, which originated in the Late Bronze Age and was used as a temple complex during the Roman period. It is a Scheduled Ancient Monument. There is nothing to see of the Second World War defended locality, but recent excavations discovered at least one L-shaped slit trench.

Directions and access

There is a car park at the top of the tank road on Springhead Hill. From here take the footpath south across the fields and at the junction of footpaths at the top of the hill turn right. The Churchill tank is lying in the field edge adjacent to the footpath after about 100m. Return to the footpath junction and turn right, follow the footpath for another 600m until a small copse is visible in the fields on your right. The destroyed emplacement is located here, but it is on private land.

Barns Farm Camp can be approached from the A283 by a road and footpath. The group of anti-tank cylinders are a little further east along the A283, adjacent to the dog kennels.

To find the two emplacements at Washington, park in the car park adjacent to the A24 south of Washington village. Cross the A24 and follow the South Downs Way west onto Highden Hill. The first emplacement is situated in a field adjacent to the South Downs Way; the second emplacement is some 500m further on, hidden in a hedge line on the south side of the South Downs Way.

Chanctonbury Ring can be reached by footpaths from a car park at the end of Chanctonbury Ring Road from the A283.

References/Background reading

Nicoll, A. 2007, 'A Churchill Exhumed', *Britain at War Magazine* No. 4, Storrington, Green Arbor Publishing Ltd, 35-41

Mace, M.F. 1997, *Sussex Wartime Relics and Memorials*, Storrington, Historic Military Press

Rudling, D. 2001, 'Chanctonbury Ring revisited', *Sussex Archaeological Collections* 139, 75-121

PRO WO 166/788, West Sussex Division: Operation Instruction No.3, 4 December 1940

SITE 19: FINDON

Period: **Nineteenth Century to Second World War**
Type of Site: **Training camps and Nodal Point**

History

The Downs around Findon were frequently used for training from the latter end of the nineteenth century through to the Second World War. In 1897 a large army camp was located in the Hill Barn area and in the early twentieth century volunteer units used the area for their annual training camps.

In 1940 Findon became a Category 'A' Nodal Point and some 391 anti-tank cubes were placed around the village. The line of cubes stretched up to Church Hill winding around the churchyard (*41*) following the line of the footpath and may have

41 Wartime photograph showing the line of anti-tank cubes that formed part of the Nodal Point defences around Findon, passing Findon Church and heading up on to Church Hill. *West Sussex County Council Library Service: PP/WSL/WGP00031*. www.westsussexpast.org.uk/picture

continued on to where a roadblock blocked the small farm track (Honeysuckle Lane) on the north side of Church Hill, near Tolmare Farm. At 'The Vale' on the A24 there was another roadblock comprising six circular concrete blocks with pyramidal tops that were placed across the road to form a narrow gap through which vehicles passed and which could be blocked with hairpin rails. A number of pillboxes were constructed and barbed wire was laid out, while a sandbagged post covered the road junction at 'The Square'. Anti-glider trenches were dug in the surrounding fields and metal poles erected to impede landing aircraft and gliders.

The Findon Manor Hotel was requisitioned as the headquarters for the defending troops and was later occupied by units from the 2nd Canadian Division. A well concealed OP was placed in a specially constructed tower amongst the trees on the summit of Church Hill.

The Iron Age hillfort at Cissbury had been used as a beacon site in 1587 at the time of the Spanish Armada and in the Napoleonic Wars may have been the location for one of a number of advanced infantry posts positioned near the south coast. In 1940 Cissbury was put into a state of all-round defence. An anti-tank ditch was excavated around the outside of the hillfort ditch, with barbed wire and other defences placed around its perimeter. A 6in gun was positioned in the fort, together with one or more anti-aircraft guns.

The sites today

There is very little evidence for the Nodal Point defences at Findon today, as they were quickly cleared after the war, with all of the cubes on Church Hill and around the church having been removed. The roadblock at the Vale was also cleared and subsequent road re-surfacing has removed the hairpin rail sockets. However, near Tolmare Farm a set of some 12 hairpin rail sockets can be seen in the surface of the farm track (TQ 1098 0875).

Cissbury is located at TQ140080; it comprises an Iron Age hillfort overlying a Neolithic flint mine complex at its western end and is a Scheduled Ancient Monument in the ownership of the National Trust. Although the filled-in anti-tank ditch around Cissbury showed as a white scar on aerial photographs taken immediately after the war, there is no trace of this on the ground today. Towards the eastern end of the hillfort interior, there are a number of earthworks, some of which are currently overgrown with gorse. An oval depression approximately 12m in diameter, with soil embanked around its outside and an entrance at its north end, has a central concrete base and may be a weapon position (TQ 1405 0823). Three other similar positions are located nearby and a further one is situated outside the hillfort on the south-east side.

Directions and access

The roadblock near Tolmare Farm can be reached by taking the A280 from the roundabout at Findon on the A24. After about 1km, park in the large entrance to Tolmare Farm and cross the road to follow the footpath along the track for about 50m. Cissbury can be reached by taking the minor road from the centre of Findon to a small car park close to the hillfort, or alternatively park in one of the car parks in Findon Valley and walk to the site. The positions within the hillfort are located close to the trig point.

References/Background reading

Donachie, J.D. & Field, D.J. 1994, 'Cissbury Ring: A Survey by the RCHME', *Sussex Archaeological Collections* 132, 25-32

www.findonvillage.com

SITE 20: BRAMBER, STEYNING AND UPPER BEEDING

Period: **English Civil War and Second World War**
Type of Site: **Castle and Nodal Point**

History

Bramber Castle was founded shortly after the Norman Conquest and was first mentioned in 1073. Initially a ditched motte, its ditch was in-filled and a curtain wall and gatehouse were erected between 1075 and 1100, whilst a deep ditch surrounded the natural mound on which it stood. By the end of the sixteenth century the castle appears to have been a ruin. During the Civil War,

Parliamentarian forces made preparations to defend Bramber against the incursion into Sussex by Lord Hopton in December 1643. There is mention of 'workes at Bramber and Shoreham being built by the pioneers' and a 'fort at Bramber' being defended against 'a bold and daring enemy' on the 12 December. However, it is not clear whether this relates to reuse of the castle as a defensive position or new defences erected by the Parliamentarian troops. There was a further encounter between Royalist Horse and Parliamentarian Dragoons at Bramber Bridge just after Christmas 1643, which resulted in a few casualties on both sides and checked the eastward advance of the Royalist forces. Prince Charles (the future Charles II) is reputed to have stayed at St Mary's House in The Street during his escape through Sussex in 1651, before setting sail for France from Shoreham.

In 1940 the area of Steyning, Bramber and Upper Beeding became a Nodal Point. At Steyning, roadblocks with hairpin rails and fixed flame defences supported by a pillbox and an anti-tank gun position were set up to cover the approaches from the west into Bramber. The fixed flame defences comprised concealed pipes on either side of the road with holes drilled in them. When required, taps would be turned on and the oil ran through the pipes from tanks concealed nearby and spilt onto the road where it was ignited. At Upper Beeding to the east of Bramber, a number of roadblocks together with a *flame fougasse* or fixed flame defence covered by pillboxes and an anti-tank gun emplacement were set up to cover the roads into the village from the south and east. At Bramber itself there was a roadblock and railblock at the railway bridge on the west side of the village, covered by pillboxes, whilst Beeding Bridge had a roadblock with a flame trap and was covered by a gun emplacement. Bramber Castle was formed into a strongpoint by the addition of two pillboxes and three infantry section posts. The fifteenth-century St Mary's House was requisitioned and used by Canadian troops until 1944.

Searchlights were positioned at Waterworks Corner on the Beeding to Henfield Road and in Market Field, Steyning, and two anti-aircraft guns were placed near Beeding Bridge with another on the lawn of 'The Towers'. Four 25pdr field guns were positioned at Castletown and a large howitzer was positioned near Steyning Bostal.

A number of surface air-raid shelters were built in the villages, with examples in Steyning at Mouse Lane, White Horse Square and Elm Grove Lane, whilst many houses had brick blast walls built in front of their doors or windows to provide additional protection. The civil defence command post for Steyning was set up in a cellar in Dog Lane.

Steyning also had an Observer Corps post. This was initially at the top of the Memorial Playing Fields, but later moved into a two-storey brick building in a field above the Bostal. After the war it moved into an underground bunker in the same field, which opened in 1959 and was closed in 1991.

To the north and south of Bramber large concrete gun emplacements covered the bridges over the River Adur. These were designed to take wheeled artillery pieces, which could be manoeuvred into the emplacement through the large

42 The open rear of the gun emplacement at Coombes (TQ 1951 0875). These were probably designed to take QF 18pdr guns or ex-USA 75mm M1917 guns

open space at the rear (*42*), while the narrow front face with a large embrasure facing the bridge gave the gun and crew some protection. Given the fact that many of the army's 25pdr field guns had been abandoned in France, it is most likely that the guns that were actually used in these emplacements in 1940 were either 75mm M1917 guns that had been supplied by the Americans in June of that year, or QF 13pdr or 18pdrs. This type of emplacement appears to be unique to West Sussex and a number can be found along the Rivers Adur and Arun.

The sites today

The ruins of Bramber Castle (TQ185107) look out over the low-lying Adur valley. Archaeological excavations at the castle have found no evidence for any building work dating to the English Civil War, or for the subsequent demolition of the castle by Parliamentarian forces, as has been suggested. There is also little evidence for the Second World War defences that were added to the castle and then subsequently removed. A short length of flint walling on the causeway (TQ 1857 1063) across the moat is pierced by three loopholes which cover the moat on the south-west side of the castle and may be part of one of the infantry section posts. On the east side of the castle two possible loopholes (one blocked) pierce the walls of the fourteenth-century building (TQ 1856 1076) and hint that this may have been utilised, as it has commanding views across the valley to the river.

Most of the remaining Second World War defences around the villages were removed soon after the war, although some pillboxes may have survived until quite recently, as at least one covering the Henfield Road (A2037) at Upper Beeding (TQ 1994 1004) was marked on the 1971 edition OS map. The gun emplacement covering Beeding Bridge was located to the north-west of the bridge (approx.

43 The above ground features (access hatch, BPI baffle plate and air vent) of the Steyning ROC Post (TQ 1738 1032)

TQ 1916 1068), but has now disappeared under the new houses that have been built here. Nothing survives of the other defences at Beeding Bridge, but the bridge retains its rather faded black and white blackout markings (*colour plate 14*).

None of the air-raid shelters in Steyning have survived, but at least one house in Church Street has the remains of a brick blast wall still in situ. Four air-raid shelters survive in Upper Beeding. The first is situated in the garden of the Rising Sun public house and is an unusual design – partly sunken with a brick blast wall and a sloping roof (TQ 1961 1034). Although oral evidence suggests that this was used as an air-raid shelter, its location and unusual design suggests that it may have originated as a machine gun emplacement. The second shelter is located behind the village hall and is a small rectangular brick shelter now used as a store (TQ 1949 1047). Other shelters apparently exist behind the old Police House in Hyde Lane and at Sele Court.

The ROC post at Steyning is located in a field off Bostal Road. A metalled track leads from the road to a field entrance and some 50m into the field there is a fenced enclosure which contains the underground bunker (TQ 1738 1032). All of the above-ground features – the access hatch, BPI baffle plate and air vent – are extant and in good condition (*43*).

South of Bramber at Coombes, a single gun emplacement covered the now demolished railway bridge over the River Adur (*colour plate 15*). Originally there would probably have been two of these gun emplacements, one on each side of the river presumably to counter potential attackers in either direction. The gun emplacement on the east bank was placed amongst the houses in Dacre Gardens, but was demolished after the war. The surviving emplacement at

Coombes is located at TQ 1951 0875 and faces south-east towards the bridge. It was originally situated on a field boundary, but today the area around it has been landscaped, blocking the view to the river and a fishing lake (Passies Ponds) has been constructed immediately to its rear.

Directions and access

Bramber Castle has its own car park, accessed from the roundabout on the A283, or there is a small car park in The Street in Bramber. To reach the castle from here, walk along The Street and take the path upslope past St Nicholas' parish church. As you cross the causeway across the moat towards the gatehouse, the loopholes are on the left. From the castle Beeding Bridge is a short walk east along The Street past St Mary's House.

To visit the air-raid shelters in Upper Beeding, park in the car park off the High Street and cross the road to see the shelter at the rear of the village hall. Follow the road past the garage to the Rising Sun, where the shelter is in the pub garden, although there may not be access to it.

The Steyning ROC post is on private farmland, but can be seen from the field gate. There is no parking nearby on Bostal Road, although there is a layby a few hundred metres further uphill.

The gun emplacement at Coombes can be found at Passies Ponds, which are reached from Coombes Road between Steyning and Shoreham.

Opening times

Bramber Castle is owned by the National Trust and is in the care of English Heritage, and can be visited at any reasonable time.

St Mary's House is open on Sundays, Thursdays and Bank Holiday Mondays, 2-6pm (last entry at 5pm), May to end of September. Tel: 01903 816205

Permission to visit the gun emplacement at Passies Ponds should be obtained from the office at the site during opening hours.

References/Background reading

Barton, K.J. & Holden, E.W. 1977, 'Excavations at Bramber Castle, Sussex, 1966-67', *Archaeological Journal* 134, 11-79

Grehan, J. 2001, *Battles & Battlefields of Sussex*, Storrington, Historic Military Press

Short, J. 2005, *The Remains of a Military Landscape*, unpublished MA thesis, University of Leicester

West, W.J. 2004, *Life in Sussex in World War Two*, Steyning Grammar School Oral History Project

PRO WO166/4630 9th Bn. Royal Welch Fusiliers Defence Scheme, September 1941.

www.stmarysbramber.co.uk

SITE 21: HENFIELD TO BOLNEY

Period: **Second World War**
Type of Site: **Nodal Points & Gun emplacements**

History

Henfield and the nearby villages of Partridge Green, Cowfold and Bolney all became Nodal Points in 1940. At Henfield the Nodal Point covered Barrow Hill and Golden Square, and there was a roadblock at the top of Bramlands Lane in Woodmancote. A number of pillboxes were built, including one at the junction of Cagefoot Lane and the High Street, one at the junction of Blackgate Lane and Cagefoot Lane, and two that can be seen on a 1946 aerial photograph along Nep Town Road and Mill End. A *flame fougasse* was set up at Barrow Hill with 40g oil drums buried in the banks. It was intended that this would be set off when enemy tanks halted to contemplate the 2m high red brick wall that blocked the road in front of them. This was actually painted on a canvas or hessian sheet, which could be stretched across the road in the event of an attack. The Home Guard had its HQ in Eardly Hall and mounted guards every night at the Windmill and at 'Hunters View' at Woodmancote. An ARP post was established in the Assembly Rooms in the High Street and a number of air-raid shelters were constructed or improvised from existing cellars. The Henfield Nodal Point was reduced in size in 1942, so that it only covered the important road junction at Golden Square.

Little is known of the Partridge Green and Cowfold Nodal Points, but the important crossroads of the A23 and A272 at Bolney meant that this was an important Nodal Point. The Home Guard at Bolney had their HQ in the village school and manned posts in the Church tower and at the Post Office each night. Their guardroom was located at 'Walnut and Well Cottage' and the armoury was at the rear of the Vicarage. A number of searchlight sites were situated around the village, including one at the A23/A272 crossroads. A garage on the London Road became a small munitions factory and possessed the only air-raid shelter in the village.

Pairs of gun emplacements were built to cover the railway and road bridges across the River Adur, continuing the Stop Line that had started at Shoreham. The railway bridges at Stretham Manor (south of Henfield), Betley Bridge (north of Henfield), the road crossings at Mock Bridge (Shermanbury) and Bines Bridge (south of Partridge Green) were all provided with gun emplacements.

Many of the gun emplacements on this stretch of the river carry an inscription, 'Ringmer Building Works Ltd 1940', etched into the concrete. This company originated as part of the Glyndebourne Estate, but later became a sizeable local building company who were contracted to build these emplacements.

A causeway was built by Canadian Engineers between the end of West End Lane and the River Adur at Henfield using rubble that had been brought by train from various blitzed cities. The causeway allowed the Engineers to practice bridge building and also added a further crossing point over the river during the build-up for D-Day.

The sites today

Nothing survives of the Nodal Point defences in any of the villages, although at Henfield five anti-tank buoys are located at the entrance to King James' Lane (TQ 2154 1554) close to the possible site of a roadblock at Barrow Hill. Also at Henfield there is a small surface air-raid shelter (*44*). This is built into the side of a twitten at the end of Park Road (TQ 2138 1594) and has an entrance (now bricked-up) in its side wall. Another shelter may survive in the grounds of Moustows Manor in the High Street (TQ 2155 1576). Although the various buildings utilised by the Home Guard and civil defence organisations survive in Bolney, there are no indications of their use surviving today.

Most of the gun emplacements along the River Adur are still in place. A gun emplacement sits alongside the disused railway line south-west of the railway bridge near Stretham Manor (TQ 1972 1324). In 1940 this was positioned in a hedgeline, facing north-east to cover the bridge; a 1946 aerial photograph shows a clear track leading to the rear of the emplacement. The gun emplacement on the east bank of the river sits in the grounds of Stretham Manor (approx. TQ 2011 1368). Further north the railway line re-crosses the river at Betley Bridge and there are two gun emplacements remaining. On the south side of the river a gun emplacement is positioned adjacent to, and on the west side of, the disused railway line (TQ 2016 1724) and faces north to cover the bridge. On the north side of the river the gun emplacement is situated on rising open ground, but on a

44 Surface air-raid shelter in Park Road, Henfield (TQ 2138 1594)

slight false crest giving it a 'hull-down' position, facing south towards the bridge (TQ 1988 1768). Both of these emplacements have turf on their roof, as an aid to their camouflage.

The River Adur then turns eastwards and is crossed by the A281 road at Mock Bridge, Shermanbury. One gun emplacement is located on the south side of the river, adjacent to the car park of the Bull Inn (TQ 2110 1814) and faces north to cover the bridge. The second emplacement is situated on the north side of the bridge, in the front edge of a copse, adjacent to the drive of Shermanbury Place. This emplacement has an inscription, 'Ringmer Building Works Ltd (Oct) 1940', on the right side wall. Two anti-tank buoys are situated at the entrance to Gratwicke (TQ 2088 2096) on the A281 between Shermanbury and Cowfold.

A branch of the River Adur joins from the west and is crossed by the B2135 at Bines Bridge, near Bines Green. One gun emplacement sits in a hedgeline on the north-west side of the bridge, set back some 40m from the river (approx. TQ189176). The second emplacement is located on the east side of the river, at the entrance to Bines Farmhouse and adjacent to a footpath (TQ 1902 1754). Although very overgrown, it is in good condition and also has a 'Ringmer Building Works Ltd' inscription on its east wall. In the layby opposite the entrance to Bines Farm there may be the concrete base of a cut-down coffin.

Along Wineham Lane there are a number of anti-tank buoys which will have originated from roadblocks in the area. Three buoys are located at the entrance to the industrial park at Greenacres Farm (TQ 2425 2264); one is at the entrance to the caravan park (TQ 2366 2078) and two white-painted buoys are situated at the entrance to Gatefield (TQ 2359 2010).

Directions and access

To find the air-raid shelter in Henfield, walk along Park Road from the High Street and at the end turn left into the twitten; the shelter is on the right.

The gun emplacements at Stretham and Betley Bridge are best reached using the Downs Link which runs along the line of the dismantled railway and can be accessed at Henfield or further north at Partridge Green. However, it is not possible to visit the gun emplacement located at Stretham Manor. The emplacement north of Betley Bridge is in a field beside the disused railway, but the emplacement south of the Bridge is overgrown and cannot be accessed. The gun emplacement on the south side of Mock Bridge is beside the car park of the Bull Inn and can be reached through the overflow car park. The emplacement on the north side of the bridge is on the right, a short distance along the drive to Shermanbury Place. The gun emplacement on the west side of Bines Bridge is not accessible, but the one on the east side is located beside the footpath at the entrance to Bines Farmhouse. Wineham Lane is on the south side of the A272 between Cowfold and Bolney.

References/Background reading

Bishop, L. 1981, *Henfield in Battledress*, Henfield, Lucie Bishop

Burgess, M., Davies, B. and George, P. 2005, *Bolney at War*, Bolney Local History Society, Burgess Hill, Ditchling Press

http://www.100megsfree.com/hhg/page8.html *Henfield's WW2 Home Guard*, Henfield History Group

SITE 22: TRULEIGH

Period: **Second World War and Cold War**
Type of Site: **Radar Station**

History

A Chain Home Low (CHL) radar station was built at Truleigh Hill in 1939 and became operational in July 1940. It was equipped with a single rotating combined transmitting and receiving aerial, and was updated with more advanced radar sets later in the war. In 1942 a GEE navigational aid was added, resulting in the construction of six tall aerials, together with receiver and transmission blocks at the site. The personnel were billeted in Shoreham.

After the war, the site was upgraded to a Chain Home Extra Low (CHEL) radar site, which was completed in 1952 with an R2 single level underground operations room and a Type 14 radar system as part of the ROTOR network. The standby set house was located at New Erringham Farm. Operations ceased in 1956 and the site was decommissioned in 1958. The domestic site for RAF Truleigh Hill was located between Stoney Lane and Buci Crescent in Shoreham and opened in 1952. It was closed in 1958, with the buildings being demolished in 1965.

Truleigh Hill was also a defended locality in 1940 and was prepared for all-round defence. It had a wired perimeter and would have been manned by a single infantry company, supplemented by four MMGs and two 2pdr anti-tank guns, all manning dug-in positions around the hill. Although referred to as Truleigh Hill, it is possible that this defended locality was actually positioned at Mill Hill (see Site 9).

The site today

After the site was decommissioned, it was sold to a private buyer in 1965. There are currently a number of radio masts located at the site for the emergency services and commercial organisations, but most of the above-ground radar station structures have now been removed.

A tarmac road leads up to the locked entrance of the compound (TQ 2250 1069). Inside there is a standard ROTOR-type guardhouse with veranda and beyond that there are two masts, whilst a further mast is situated within a modern

45 The blast wall for the eastern (T2) GEE transmitter block at Truleigh Hill. The gap in the side wall is modern, and the structure has been converted for agricultural use

compound on the north side. A small brick building with a concrete roof is situated on the east side of the main compound and is probably the base building of the Type 14 Mk 7 aerial for the CHEL system. On the west side and outside the compound is an air vent for the underground bunker. A concrete building base is situated outside the compound on its east side, but there are no indications of other structures here.

A short distance further east, just before reaching Truleigh Hill Barn, there is a white brick structure that has been converted to agricultural use (TQ 2264 1064). This is actually the blast wall for the eastern (T2) GEE transmitter block, although all the internal structure has been removed. It is rectangular with a staggered entrance (now blocked) at the south end (*45*) and there appears to have been a similar entrance at the north end. The opening in the west side wall is modern, but allows you to see the metal reinforcement rods in the brick wall structure.

In the field to the north of Truleigh Hill Barn there is an octagonal direction-finding fixer tower (TQ 2273 1076). This comprises an octagonal white brick structure with a rendered surface, sitting on top of a square plinth. The plinth is made from red bricks topped with a concrete 'roof' on which sits two courses of white brick set in a square, with the octagonal structure on top. On the west side there is a brick passage which may enclose steps down to a below-ground entrance and there are also three steps up to the octagonal structure. A metal pipe runs from the north end of this passage to a rectangular concrete structure some 7m further north, which may be the base for a small building.

This octagonal tower is similar to, although smaller than, the towers found on Halnaker Hill (Site 12); these were topped by a wooden structure which contained the radio direction-finding equipment and it is likely that this tower had a similar structure on top as well.

The standby set house at New Erringham Farm has been converted into a residence (TQ214083). Nothing survives of the domestic site in Shoreham.

Directions and access

To get to Truleigh Hill, you need to take Mill Lane from Shoreham. Follow this for 4km and park in the car park at Beeding Hill. From here walk east along the South Downs Way past Tottington Barn YHA and the row of houses. The entrance to the compound is up the tarmac road on the left; although there is no access to the site itself, the guardhouse and other features inside the compound can be seen from the entrance. Continue east towards Truleigh Hill Barn where the transmitter block blast wall can be seen on the left just before reaching the barn. The direction-finding fixer tower can be seen in the field behind the barn, but there is no public access to these sites. Marlipins Museum at 36 High Street, Shoreham has a display and information on RAF Truleigh Hill.

Opening times

Marlipins Museum is open Tuesday-Saturday 2 May-31 October, and also on Bank Holiday Mondays (May-October): 10.30am-4.30pm. Tel: 01273 462994

References/Background reading

Haigh, J.D. Brig. 1960, *The Services Textbook of Radio*, Volume 7, Radiolocation Techniques, London, H.M.S.O.

Taylor, R. 2007, *Shoreham's Radar Station: The Story of RAF Truleigh Hill*, privately published

SITE 23: BURGESS HILL, HASSOCKS AND HURSTPIERPOINT

Period: **Second World War**
Type of Site: **Nodal Points**

History

The small mid-Sussex town of Burgess Hill and nearby villages of Hassocks and Hurstpierpoint all became Category 'A' Nodal Points in 1940. Roadblocks were positioned at bridges across the Heron Stream, a tributary of the River Adur, to the south of Burgess Hill.

At Hurstpierpoint, there were defence posts at Lock's Manor, College Lane and near the fire station. Danny House was used for high level planning meetings, whilst Canadian soldiers were billeted around the village and Commandos carried out their training on the Danny Estate. The cellars of the brewery and the adjacent Sussex Arms were used as air-raid shelters by the school children.

Searchlights and anti-aircraft guns were stationed in the area, with a searchlight initially located at Lunces Hall south of Burgess Hill, then later moved nearer to Griggs. Another searchlight was positioned near Pakyns at Hurstpierpoint, with some anti-aircraft guns nearby. An anti-aircraft battery and searchlight was located in a field at the north end of Grand Avenue, Hassocks.

In Hassocks the Council School (now the Infants School) had separate air-raid shelters for boys and girls and the Adastra Hut was used as the ARP control room. In Burgess Hill there was an ARP wardens post in Cyprus Road.

The sites today

Almost nothing survives of the Nodal Point defences in the three settlements, but there is evidence for the roadblocks located at two bridges across the Heron Stream. The first roadblock is situated on the A273 at Hammonds Mill between Hassocks and Burgess Hill, where two anti-tank coffins are still in situ on the north bank of the stream (*46*), on the west side of the road (TQ 3054 1737). There are also two anti-tank buoys at the entrance to Clayton Priory, 400m north of the bridge (TQ 3066 1780). The second roadblock is at the bridge at Ruckford Mill on the minor road between Hurstpierpoint and Burgess Hill (TQ 2922 1818). There is a single anti-tank coffin on the north side of the stream on the east side of the road, with two anti-tank buoys discarded in the stream below it.

There are two painted anti-tank buoys sitting at the entrance to Bridge Hall Cottage, north of Burgess Hill, on the B2036 to Ansty. Along Bishopstone Lane to

46 The two surviving anti-tank coffins at Hammonds Mill, Burgess Hill (TQ 3054 1737)

the west of Burgess Hill there are two anti-tank cylinders and some 12 anti-tank buoys on the side of the road opposite Hilder Farm (TQ 2855 2224).

Directions and access

The Hammonds Mill roadblock is on the A273 between Hassocks and Burgess Hill. Park in the layby near Clayton Priory and walk to the bridge along the footpath. There is no access to the coffins, but they can be clearly seen from the verge and the footpath on the opposite bank of the stream. There is no parking place near the roadblock at Ruckford Mill, but the coffin and buoys can be seen from the bridge.

References/Background reading

Jones, D. 2001, *Hassocks*, Hassocks, Clayton Consultancy Ltd

Nelson, I. (ed.) 2001, *Hurstpierpoint – Kind and Charitable*, Burgess Hill, Ditchling Press Ltd

Stevens, B. undated, *Albourne 1901-2000*, Hove, Delta Press

Warne, H. (ed.) 1994, *Wivelsfield: The History of a Wealden Parish*, Hurstpierpoint, Pier Point Publishing

SITE 24: SCAYNES HILL TO HAYWARDS HEATH

Period: **English Civil War and Second World War**
Type of Site: **Pillboxes and roadblocks**

History

In 1642, local Royalist forces under Edward Ford, the Sheriff of Sussex, who were advancing on Lewes, were met by a smaller Parliamentarian force at Haywards Heath. After a short engagement, probably on the higher ground where the church now stands, the Royalist forces were routed and fled from the battlefield.

During the Second World War, a Corps Stop Line followed the line of the River Ouse west from Uckfield through into West Sussex and then on to Guildford in Surrey. This line was not as strongly protected as the GHQ Stop Line; its defences were instead concentrated at the bridges over the River Ouse. Each bridge was provided with anti-tank coffins and other blocks such as cylinders and buoys, whilst Type 28 anti-tank pillboxes and Type 24 pillboxes, usually one of each type at each bridge, were constructed to defend these crossing points. The river was modified by cutting the north bank vertically and revetting it with wooden piles and brushwood, all of which was done manually by local contractors under military supervision.

Haywards Heath was a Category 'B' Nodal Point and there were roadblocks around the centre of the town, with anti-tank pimples at the junction of the

47 Type 28A anti-tank pillbox covering the roadblock at Lindfield Bridge (TQ 3525 2631)

Broadway and South Road, and in Haywards Road. The 13th Sussex (Haywards Heath) Home Guard Battalion had an OP in the church tower.

The sites today

There are elements of two surviving roadblocks and their associated defences on this stretch of the River Ouse. The first is located at Freshfield Mill where a single overgrown coffin sits on a large concrete base on the north-west side of Freshfield Bridge (TQ 3851 2448). Nearby there are a number of partly buried anti-tank cylinders along the edge of the old canal (TQ 3841 2446) on the road to the sewage works opposite The Sloop public house. An anti-tank buoy sits in the pub car park. There are no indications of any pillboxes covering the bridge at Freshfield or at East Mascalls Bridge (TQ 3654 2543), however, it is almost certain that pillboxes would have been constructed here.

At Lindfield Bridge, north of Haywards Heath, there are two coffins on the south-east side of the bridge (TQ 3522 2627), with a Type 28A anti-tank pillbox located a short distance further north (TQ 3525 2631). The Type 28A has an anti-tank gun compartment on its west side with an embrasure facing south towards the bridge (47). An internal blast wall separates this from the machine gun compartment, which has embrasures in the south and east walls. There is an external blast wall protecting the rear entrance. This pillbox appears to be badly sited, as it is not possible to see the road from the south approaching the bridge and any vehicle crossing the bridge would appear without warning some 50m in front of the pillbox. A Type 24 pillbox may have been located on the west side of the road, but appears to have been demolished.

Near Great Haywards in Haywards Heath, there are 27 anti-tank cylinders that have been used to create a wall (TQ 3264 2358) and must have originated from a nearby roadblock.

Directions and access

Freshfield Bridge is situated some 2km along Nash Lane to Danehill and Horsted Keynes from Scaynes Hill on the A272. Park in The Sloop car park. The coffin is located at the river bridge, not the canal bridge, and is difficult to see in summer.

Lindfield Bridge is located north of Lindfield on the B2028 to Ardingly. There is a small layby on the side of the road between the bridge and the Type 28A pillbox. The pillbox is beside the road and can be accessed through a gate to the adjacent footpath.

The anti-tank cylinders at Great Haywards are on private property with no access.

References/Background reading

Rogers, L. 1999, *Haywards Heath – Yesterday Remembered*, Chichester, RPM Reprographics Ltd

SITE 25: ARDINGLY

Period: **Second World War**
Type of Site: **Nodal Point, pillboxes and Zero Station**

History

The Corps Stop Line continued to follow the line of the River Ouse west from Lindfield (Site 24) to the south of Ardingly and then on to Slaugham (Site 26). The Stop Line defences were concentrated at the bridges over the River Ouse, with each bridge being provided with anti-tank coffins and other blocks such as cylinders and buoys, and covered by Type 28 anti-tank pillboxes and Type 24 pillboxes. The banks of the River Ouse were modified to improve their ability to act as an anti-tank ditch. The north bank was cut straight and then revetted with wooden wattles held in place by wooden poles windlassed back tightly to the bank. All of this work was done manually by a group of 70-80 locally hired workmen, using trees cut down from around the river, which also helped to improve defensive fields of fire.

Ardingly, and Balcombe to its west, were both designated as Nodal Points. At Ardingly the Home Guard used the Greyhound public house as their HQ, with an OP at 'Lullings' on West Hill. The four roads into the centre of the village had roadblocks with anti-tank cylinders and/or buoys, supplemented with Dannert wire; a wire perimeter fence was erected around the main part of the village. Some trenches were dug and houses nominated as defensive positions in the event of an attack. The ARP HQ was located at 'Bawtry' with a second post at the Post Office. The school air-raid shelter was in the basement of the Rectory. Around Ardingly anti-glider posts were erected in the fields to the south and east and there were two searchlights located to the north of the village. Some anti-aircraft guns were positioned near Ardingly College and others to the north of the village. Ardingly railway station was used for the building and storage of shuttering that would be used in the construction of pillboxes in the surrounding area.

Wakehurst Place was used by the army during the war, but a more secretive installation, called a Zero Station, was built in the grounds of the mansion. A Zero Station was intended to receive coded information from Special Duties Organisation operatives who would be spying on German forces in the event of an invasion. The Zero Station, which was manned by women of the ATS, would then pass on this information via a direct phone line to the Special Duties HQ at Hannington Hall, Wiltshire.

The sites today

There is nothing surviving of the Nodal Point defences at Ardingly, although many of the buildings that would have been used as defensive positions are still present and the Home Guard HQ (Greyhound) is now called 'The Ardingly Inn'.

At Lower Ryelands Bridge between Haywards Heath and Ardingly, there is a single overgrown anti-tank coffin located on the south-west side of the bridge (TQ 3405 2720). About 100m north-west of the bridge there is a Type 28A anti-tank pillbox built into the slope (TQ 3401 2730), facing towards the bridge. It has a holdfast for a 6pdr gun and chamfered corners, with one at the rear having a machine gun embrasure incorporated, there is also an external blast wall. The chamfered corners also feature a decorative pattern of red bricks, which must have formed part of the camouflage, perhaps with a dummy pitched roof to make it look like a farm building. A Type 24 variant pillbox also covers this bridge and is located about 600m east of the bridge on a bend in the river (TQ 3463 2715). It apparently has some wartime graffiti, but it was not possible to verify this as permission to visit the site could not be obtained.

The Haywards Heath to Balcombe road crosses the River Ouse at Upper Ryelands Bridge, whilst 100m west of the bridge, the Ouse Valley Viaduct carries the London to Brighton railway line across the valley. There are no surviving coffins and there's no other evidence of a roadblock here, but three pillboxes were built to cover this important point. A Type 28A pillbox sits on a large concrete base beside a stream in a small wood north of the bridge (TQ 3241 2813). It has an L-shaped external blast wall with steps down to enter the interior at the side of the pillbox. The anti-tank compartment has a 6pdr holdfast and faces both the road bridge and the viaduct. The machine gun compartment is unusual in that the embrasure is in an angled corner wall facing south-east and still has its wooden shelf sitting on brick supports.

48 Type 24 pillbox at Upper Rylands Bridge (TQ 3194 2788), showing the 'L'-shaped external blast wall at the entrance

The second pillbox is situated some 400m further east and is partly sunken into the slope about 30m north of the river (TQ 3279 2816). The pillbox is very overgrown, but appears to be a Type 24 (thin-walled or squashed) variant with steps down to a covered entrance in a sidewall. There are four embrasures, one of which still has its wooden shelf on brick supports, and an internal blast wall. The final pillbox is a Type 24 (*48*); it is situated on the east side of the railway viaduct and was originally in a field boundary (TQ 3194 2788). It has an L-shaped external blast wall leading to an entrance in the rear wall and inside there are five pre-cast embrasures each with a semi-circular concrete machine gun table (*49*).

Further west, two roads cross the River Ouse and the bridges are each covered by a Type 28A pillbox. The first is built into the slope of a hill near Pilstye Farm (TQ 3075 2831) and faces south-east to cover the bridge on the B2036 (*colour plate 16*). Protecting the entrance is an external blast wall constructed from a different coloured brick, which has been added later. There are also some wire clips on the roof, which presumably held the camouflage in place. The second Type 28A is located near Spicers Farm (approx. TQ303282) and faces south-east to cover Cherry Lane Bridge.

The Zero Station is situated in the grounds of Wakehurst Place (TQ 3376 3125). It comprises an underground chamber constructed from corrugated iron on a concrete base, resembling a Nissen hut, with a vertical access shaft at one

49 The semi-circular concrete machine gun tables and pre-cast embrasures inside the Type 24 pillbox at Upper Rylands Bridge

end. At the opposite end is an escape tunnel, formed from pre-cast concrete pipe sections, which turns to the west and after 17m emerges in the edge of a quarry. On a site visit in 2006 there had been some subsidence around the access shaft and the underground chamber shows as a slight bump in the grass. The end of the escape tunnel can be seen emerging in the quarry from below the path to the west of the chamber. In the large oak tree beside the chamber the aerial cable can be seen in a cut groove in the trunk terminating about 3m above ground level.

Directions and access

Lower Ryelands Bridge is on the road from Haywards Heath to Ardingly (High Beech Lane/College Lane). There is a small layby near the bridge from which the coffin can be visited. However, although the Type 28A can be seen during the winter months north-west of the bridge, there is no access to it or to the Type 24 variant on the east side of the bridge.

Upper Ryelands Bridge is on the Haywards Heath to Balcombe road (Bordehill Lane). There is a small layby near the bridge, but all three pillboxes are on private farmland and there is no access to any of them without obtaining permission first. The remaining two Type 28A pillboxes are both near footpaths. The one at Pilstye Farm can be seen from the adjacent footpath after passing through the farm, whilst the pillbox near Spicers Farm is not accessible.

The Zero Station at Wakehurst Place is located on the south-west side of the mansion. Cross the lawns heading for Westwood Valley, the chamber can be found situated beside a path just before the downhill incline into the dale. The chamber and oak tree are on the left of the path and the emergency exit emerges under the path into the edge of the quarry on the right. Due to the recent subsidence the site is currently fenced off, although the National Trust was intending to put up a display board.

Opening times
Wakehurst Place is owned by the National Trust and is open daily from 10am to 6pm, March to the end of October and 10am to 4.30pm November to the end of February. Tel: 01444 894000

References/Background reading

Angell, S. 1996, *The Secret Sussex Resistance*, Midhurst, Middleton Press
Maclean, A. (ed.) 1999, *A Sussex Village at War*, Ardingly Evacuee Experience Committee
Simmonds, L. undated, *My time as a Teenager in the Ardingly L.D.V.* (Home Guard), unpublished

SITE 26: SLAUGHAM

Period: **Second World War**
Type of Site: **Anti-tank ditch, pillboxes and roadblocks**

History

After passing south of Ardingly (Site 25) the Corps Stop Line followed the River Ouse west to Slaugham, where it incorporated the lake at Slaugham Place and then turned north following the Ouse (which was improved by cutting the sides straight) to Furnace Pond at Slaugham Common. From here an anti-tank ditch was dug to continue the Stop Line north to Carterslodge Pond where the Stop Line then picked up the Golding Stream, which flows westwards to become a tributary of the River Arun.

The Stop Line defences were again concentrated to cover the bridges over the River Ouse, with each bridge being provided with anti-tank coffins together with cylinders and buoys. Most bridges were covered by a Type 28 anti-tank pillbox and often supplemented by other pillboxes, mostly Type 24s, but occasionally other varieties. The recently in-filled anti-tank ditch can be traced on a 1946 aerial photograph heading north from Furnace Pond across 'The Park', then stopping at the B2110 Lower Beeding to Handcross road, where a roadblock covered by a Type 28A pillbox was situated. The anti-tank ditch then continued alongside Carterslodge Lane before stopping just short of Carterslodge Pond, with the gap between the anti-tank ditch and the pond blocked by some anti-tank coffins. Many of the pillboxes on this stretch of the line were built by the local contractor Fowler Brothers of Cowfold.

50 Partly sunken Type 24 pillbox at Staplefield Road Bridge (TQ 2720 2758); note the turf camouflage on roof

The sites today

Following the Stop Line from east to west, the first surviving roadblock is located at Hammerhill Bridge on the B2114, where there are two overgrown anti-tank coffins on the south-east side of the bridge (TQ 2819 2743). A short distance to the north-west of the bridge is a Type 24 pillbox sitting in a hedgeline (approx. TQ 2795 2752) and facing south to cover the bridge. There are no surviving coffins at the bridge on Staplefield Road, but 60m west of the bridge is a partly sunken Type 24 pillbox that sits at a bend on the north bank of the River Ouse (TQ 2720 2758) and faces south-east towards the bridge. It has a partly collapsed external blast wall with steps down into the interior of the pillbox. The roof has been covered with turf to aid its camouflage (*50*). South of here, five anti-tank cylinders are positioned at the entrance to Great Thorndean Farm on the B2115 (TQ 2698 2596).

Covering the A23 London-Brighton road bridge over the river are two Type 28A pillboxes. The first is situated to the east of the bridge (approx. TQ 2675 2776) and has a small anti-tank embrasure with a 6pdr holdfast; the machine gun chamber has three embrasures including one in a corner wall. This pillbox also covers an adjacent roadblock across a small farm bridge. The roadblock has two coffins, one on each side of the bridge; the first has a vertical slot and the second a vertical recess to take a horizontal metal rail that would have blocked the bridge (TQ 2675 2775). At the entrance to Home Farm there are two anti-tank buoys surviving from five that were previously recorded here (TQ 2683 2807). The second Type 28A is situated on the west side of the road in a field boundary behind a ditch (TQ 2636 2789) and faces south-east to cover the bridge. It has a large embrasure with a 6pdr holdfast and three machine gun embrasures; there is a detached external brick blast wall with buttresses and two small embrasures protecting the rear entrance.

At Slaugham Place there is a partly sunken Type 24 pillbox covering the bridge on the small road to Slaugham Manor. The pillbox is well camouflaged, being set low in the ground in front of the boundary hedge to Slaugham Place, and has turf covering its roof (approx. TQ 2608 2780). It has an external L-shaped brick blast wall, and inside there are wooden shelves on brick supports still in situ. At the north end of the lake at Slaugham Place there are four anti-tank coffins at a small bridge (TQ 2577 2778) blocking the gap between the lake and the deep cut on its north side. There are two coffins on each side of the bridge, but two are very overgrown and difficult to find. A little further north is an overgrown Type 24 pillbox (TQ 2578 2783) which faces south to cover this roadblock. This pillbox has an external brick blast wall and steps down, however the entrance is blocked by a gate, so there is no access to the interior.

At Slaugham Lane Bridge there are four anti-tank coffins sitting on large concrete bases (TQ 2516 2745). These would have formed part of a roadblock at this crossing over the River Ouse. Two coffins are positioned on the south-west side of the bridge and two are on the north-east side (*colour plate 17*); there is an anti-tank buoy in the edge of the stream on the east side of the bridge. A short distance to the north-east and sitting in a hedgeline is a Type 24 pillbox (TQ 2521 2570). This faces south-west towards the bridge and has an external blast wall protecting the entrance.

In the woods alongside Slaugham Lane, between the bridge and Furnace Pond, there is an unusual two-storey pillbox (TQ 2496 2788). It sits beside a stream at the bottom of a slope, facing west, and appears to have been raised to two storeys to provide a field of fire north and south along the frontage of the wood (*colour plate 18*). However, it is not high enough to look over the top of the slope to the west, although there may have been a short stretch of anti-tank ditch on this side. The pillbox has the ground plan of a Type 24, with a slightly off-set entrance in its long rear wall and an L-shaped internal blast wall. There are no embrasures on the ground floor, but next to the entrance is an opening in the ceiling to the second floor and an iron ladder. On the second floor there is a central blast wall, and five small embrasures, each originally having a set of six concrete semi-circular tables below, although only one set now survives (*51*). A second pillbox nearby faces north to cover the road crossing the south end of Furnace Pond and is almost buried. It has an 8ft entrance tunnel with a protective lip to prevent flooding (approx. TQ249280), however, this pillbox could not be located in 2007. At the south end of Furnace Pond there are 56 anti-tank buoys lining the verge (TQ 2486 2805 to TQ 2504 2806). These are not in their original location, but have been moved here from nearby roadblocks after the war and a chain-link fence has then been added to form a barrier along the edge of the road.

There is no trace of the anti-tank ditch surviving between Furnace Pond and the B2110, where a roadblock was positioned. However, at the point the anti-tank

51 The unusual multiple semi-circular concrete machine gun table below one of the five embrasures on the second storey of the two-storey pillbox at Slaugham

ditch stops, just short of the B2110 road, there are seven anti-tank coffins set at an oblique angle blocking the gap between the end of the ditch and the road (TQ 2465 2909). On the north side of the road a further seven anti-tank coffins, in a line, fill the gap between the road and the continuation of the anti-tank ditch. Both sets of coffins incorporate existing trees into their alignments. About 50m into Warren Wood from the coffins is a Type 28A pillbox (TQ 2461 2913) which faces south to cover the roadblock. It has a holdfast for a 6pdr gun and three machine gun embrasures, together with an external brick blast wall. Two of the machine gun embrasures with in situ wooden shelves are located in the west side of the pillbox to cover the anti-tank ditch, with one being in an angled north-west corner wall.

The anti-tank ditch then runs along the east side of Carterslodge Lane, where it can clearly be seen today, surviving to 1m deep and 4-5m wide, with a bank on the east side up to 3m high. It stops just short of Carterslodge Pond, where five anti-tank coffins close the gap between the end of the ditch and the pond (TQ 2427 2939) (*52*). Across the pond dam and partly terraced into the north slope of the river valley is an unusual Type 26 variant pillbox (TQ 2424 2934) which faces south across the valley to cover the road crossing the pond dam and the river to its front. It has an external blast wall forming a protective passageway into the east wall, covered by a small embrasure in the north wall of the pillbox. There are two main embrasures facing south and west with in situ wooden shelves sitting on brick supports below.

A little further west along the river there is another small bridge and although it does not appear to have been covered by a pillbox, the bridge has been blocked

52 These five anti-tank coffins block the gap between Carterslodge Pond (TQ 2427 2939) and the end of the anti-tank ditch along Carterslodge Lane

by anti-tank coffins (TQ 2389 2930). The eastern coffin has a slot through it, whilst the west coffin has a recess, into which a metal girder between the two coffins would have been placed. The central coffin has no slot and its position has blocked the space between the two other coffins, suggesting that this coffin was added later when a decision to completely block the bridge had been made.

Directions and access

Parking is difficult at Hammerhill Bridge on the B2114 south of Staplefield, but the overgrown coffins can be seen at the bridge, although the nearby pillbox is on private farmland. There is a small pull-in near the Staplefield Bridge and while the pillbox can be seen from the road, it too is on private land, although a gap in the fence used by dog walkers may provide some access. The roadblock and Type 28A pillbox south of Home Farm near the A23 are also on private farmland and cannot be visited.

The pillboxes at Slaugham Place are best reached by parking near the church in Slaugham village and then following the footpath south through the churchyard. The Type 24 pillbox is adjacent to the footpath, which then continues through a gate and over the bridge beside the lake with the anti-tank coffins. Footpaths then take you around Slaugham Place, where it is possible to see the well camouflaged semi-sunken Type 24 against the hedge of Slaugham Place, whilst the Type 28A can be seen from the road to Slaugham Manor. The roadblock and pillbox at Slaugham Lane Bridge can also be reached by a footpath from Slaugham Village, as there is no parking place nearby.

There is a small car park at the south end of Furnace Pond, from where the anti-tank buoys lining the road can be seen. To find the two-storey pillbox, walk along Slaugham Lane for about 100m, then turn into the wood on the west side of the road. The pillbox is about 30m into the wood and on the far side of a stream. Extreme caution should be exercised in climbing up the ladder into the upper floor and a torch is essential.

To see the sites near Carterslodge, it is best to park in the layby on the A279 beside Carterslodge Lane (note that the lane itself is a private road). The anti-tank coffins are at the junction between Carterslodge Lane and the A279. Follow the bridleway along Carterslodge Lane, the Type 28A pillbox is in the wood on your right after some 50m. Continue along the lane, noting the anti-tank ditch on your right, to the pond dam where the coffins are on the right. Cross the dam and enter the wood on the left side where you will see the Type 26 pillbox in front of you. Return to the lane, continue to follow it for a further 300m and then take the footpath on the left. Follow this across the field and then downslope into the wood until you reach the footbridge with the three coffins.

References/Background reading

Mace, M.F. 1996, *Frontline Sussex: The Defence Lines of West Sussex 1939-1945*, Storrington, Historic Military Press

SITE 27: HORSHAM

Period: **Napoleonic to Cold War**
Type of site: **Barracks, Drill Hall, Nodal Point and ROC HQ**

History

As one of the measures to help counter the threat of a French invasion, a large barracks was built at Horsham in 1796. It comprised eight two-storey wooden buildings in two rows of four on either side of a parade ground, sleeping 60 soldiers on each floor. At one end of the parade ground there was the officers accommodation and kitchens, with a hospital, magazine, stables and a guardhouse. Some later buildings, for example the Armoury, were more substantial brick buildings.

The Drill Hall in Denne Road, Horsham, was opened in 1927 and was initially used by the 4th Battalion of the Royal Sussex Regiment, part of the Territorial Army. During the Cold War, the HQ Company of 7th Battalion (subsequently 6/7th Battalion) of The Queens Regiment (which had incorporated the Sussex Regiment) was based there, until it became part of the Princess of Wales' Royal Regiment. To the rear of the Drill Hall were a number of ancillary buildings, including stores and garages located around a car park and grassed area. Originally these were wooden and brick buildings, but the G1098 Stores and MT garage were replaced with modern buildings during the heightened Cold War tension of the 1980s. The Drill Hall was finally closed in 1999 as part of defence cuts to the reserve forces.

In 1940 Horsham was declared a Nodal Point and a defended area was created around the core of the town. Roadblocks using large concrete cubes were established on the roads into the town, including on the Guildford Road at Farthings Hill. A later map from 28 March 1942 shows the location of weapons pits, roadblocks and defended localities.

Horsham public air-raid shelters

Location of Shelter	**Capacity (people)**
Carfax (between bandstand and memorial)	50
Adjoining The Capitol (Cinema)	200
Island in the Causeway	50
East Street car park	150
South Street car park	50
Bishopric	100
Adjoining The Star public house	150

Seven large public surface air-raid shelters were initially constructed in the town, providing shelter for 750 people, whilst additional shelters were added later and others were built at the town's schools. In early 1942, many of the surface shelters around the town were strengthened. The ARP HQ was in the basement of Park House and seven wardens posts were established around the town in 1939. A number of first aid party posts were built and the Stanley Street depot was used as a decontamination centre, whilst a number of EWS static water tanks were built to aid the fire service. Observer Corps posts were set up on the roofs of buildings in Middle Street and in Depot Road.

The Corps Stop Line followed the River Arun from Mannings Heath along the southern outskirts of Horsham, where it was integrated into the town's defence scheme and then continued on south of Broadbridge Heath to Slinfold (Site 28). The river was widened and strengthened and the banks were covered with barbed wire entanglements, whilst the bridges had roadblocks and were covered by pillboxes.

At the Hammer Pond (east of Mannings Heath) there was a roadblock covered by a pillbox and a short distance further north at Bucks Head a *flame fougasse* was built into the south bank of the road. At Golding's Bridge near Mannings Heath, the river was dredged, with the north bank being cut vertically and the south bank being cleared of undergrowth and trees and then graded to provide a more gentle slope into the river. A brick dam was also built west of the bridge to ensure the water level was kept at a reasonable height. The bridge itself had four anti-tank coffins, hairpin rail sockets and a *flame fougasse* was positioned a little further west along the road. A pillbox covered the bridge from the west and was itself covered by trenches on the ridge above.

At Faygate, a few miles north-east of Horsham, No. 49 MU RAF was established in 1940 to salvage wrecked aircraft. The aircraft were collected from across Sussex by local haulage contractor A.V. Nicholls & Co and taken to Faygate where they were broken up. The location of the MU adjacent to the railway goods yard ensured that material could then be taken away and recycled.

During the Cold War, the HQ of the ROC No. 2 Group was located to the rear of the Drill Hall in Denne Road (TQ 1740 3029). This large nuclear-proof bunker was opened in April 1962 and operated until 1992 when it was closed with the winding down of the ROC operations.

The sites today

There is no evidence for the 1796 barracks, as the site has now been covered with houses. The barracks was located between the Worthing Road and the cricket club, who now use 'Barrack Field'. The Armoury was demolished in the 1950s, with the two cannon from its entrance now in Horsham Museum. Other buildings from the barracks were taken down and reused elsewhere, with examples still in use as Charnwood Chapel and Leonardslee Lodge.

Following the Corps Stop Line westwards from Slaugham, there is a Type 26 variant pillbox covering the bridge over the river at the Hammer Pond dam (TQ 2191 2891). The pillbox is located on the west side of the bridge and is partly sunken into the bank of the river. It has short north and west walls which are connected by a short angled wall, with a small embrasure covering the entrance to the external brick blast wall. The main embrasure faces the bridge and still has a wooden shelf on brick supports below. There is the base of a cut-down anti-tank coffin on the east side of the bridge adjacent to the pond (TQ 2194 2896) and two anti-tank buoys in the river nearby – all remnants of the roadblock that was positioned at the bridge. A concrete glacis appears to have been added to the west side of the bridge to make it difficult for tanks to climb the bank. North of Mannings Heath there is a 'squashed' Type 24 pillbox partly sunk into a bank close to the river at Golding's Bridge (TQ 2066 2929). It has an external concrete blast wall with steps down into the pillbox and the roof has been covered with turf to aid its camouflage (*53*). Inside there are three embrasures with a continuous wooden shelf sitting on brick supports below and an internal blast wall. Interestingly, it appears to face across the river, rather than towards Golding's Bridge, where the roadblock has been removed as a result of bridge widening since the war. The brick dam can also be seen in the river about 20m north of the bridge (TQ 2071 2928). Further along Golding Lane there are four anti-tank buoys at 'The Goldings' (TQ 2103 2957).

A pillbox stood at Birchen Bridge on the A281 (approx. TQ 1932 2923) until the 1950s when it was demolished. A thin-walled Type 24 pillbox is located on

53 A 'squashed' Type 24 pillbox was partly sunk into a bank close to the river at Golding's Bridge (TQ 2066 2929). It has an external concrete blast wall with steps down into the pillbox, and the roof has been covered with turf to aid its camouflage

54 Thin-walled Type 24 pillbox located on the north-east side of White's Bridge, near Horsham (TQ 1876 2928). This has a raised superstructure as it is revetted into the bank

the north-east side of White's Bridge (TQ 1876 2928) and faces south to cover the bridge. Due to it being built into the slope, it has a raised brick-shuttered concrete superstructure at the front and sides (*54*) and an external blast wall at the rear. Inside there are three embrasures and a standard blast wall. Although the

55 Two anti-tank cylinders in the River Arun in Denne Road, Horsham (TQ 1709 3003). There are a number of other cylinders nearby

pillbox is brick-shuttered, part of the rear wall has been shuttered with wood. Following the river around the southern outskirts of Horsham, the first surviving defences are covering Chesworth Lane Bridge (TQ 1742 2995). There are three anti-tank pimples on the north-west side of the bridge, with at least one surviving in the garden on the south-west side and two others displaced into the river. There are also two anti-tank cylinders hidden in the undergrowth nearby. Covering the bridge is a Type 28A anti-tank pillbox (TQ 1728 2986), which now sits in a private garden. At the south end of Denne Road, at the entrance to Denne Park, there are six anti-tank cylinders (TQ 1709 2997), with another two in the river (55) near the railway bridge (TQ 1709 3003) and one more on the east side of the road bridge. In The Causeway (TQ 1718 3044) there are the cut-off roots of 29 anti-tank pimples that originally blocked the access from the river into the town from this direction. A second Type 28 anti-tank pillbox is positioned on the north side of the river covering the approach along the Worthing Road (TQ 1689 3029). The pillbox entrance and embrasures are blocked and it is covered with ivy.

On the west side of Horsham there is a single Type 24 pillbox (TQ 1536 2993), possibly the remaining one of a pair covering a farm bridge. It had been painted with a lime-green paint in a wavy pattern to camouflage it. Another bridge nearby has a single anti-tank coffin sitting on a large concrete base on the south side of the river (TQ 1504 3000), with a second coffin having probably fallen into the river due to erosion. Further west is a Type 24 pillbox built into a low bank on the edge of High Wood (TQ 1482 2985), facing east across the stream (*colour plate 19*). It has a long external blast wall with a sloping buttress at the outer end. Inside there are four pre-cast embrasures of which three have surviving semi-circular concrete tables; the fifth embrasure, in the rear north wall, is much smaller and has no table.

Mill Bridge, near Broadbridge Farm, has two uprooted anti-tank coffins (TQ 1431 3033) and is protected by an ivy-covered Type 28A anti-tank pillbox that sits at the end of a garden, at TQ 1447 3034. New Bridge on the Five Oaks Road is also covered by a Type 28A pillbox positioned in the trees alongside the road to Lower Broadbridge Farm (TQ 1400 3104). The pillbox has a main embrasure with a 6pdr holdfast, together with a single machine gun embrasure, both of which face south-west towards the bridge. A single overgrown anti-tank coffin is positioned at the bridge at Lower Broadbridge Farm (TQ140313).

The Drill Hall is owned by Horsham District Council and survives today due to its continued use as a community centre (*56*). The Drill Hall fronts onto Denne Road and a number of the original and later associated buildings survive at its rear. Some buildings are still utilised by the Army Cadet Corps and Air Training Corps, but some redevelopment of the land is now taking place. Sadly the ROC building was demolished in November 2004 and there is now no surviving trace of this important building. Due to the major redevelopment of Horsham town centre, none of the Second World War civil defence installations survive, although Park House is situated on the east side of Horsham Park (TQ 1761 3085).

The site of the MU at Faygate is now a timber yard (TQ 2170 3450), but there are parts of the site still surviving. At the entrance there are two workshop/store buildings, now re-clad with timber boarding, and a little further on beside a large corrugated iron building there is a surface air-raid shelter, now much altered and damaged (TQ 2169 3452).

56 The front of the Drill Hall, Denne Road, Horsham

Directions and access

There is very limited parking near the Hammer Pond, which is on Hammerpond Road between the B2110 and Horsham; although the cut-down coffin can be seen at the edge of the road, there is no access to the pillbox, which is on the edge of the golf course. Continue along Hammerpond Road to 'The Goldings' where the anti-tank buoys can be seen on the corner; turn into Golding Lane and park in the layby adjacent to Golding's Bridge. Cross the stile to find the pillbox close to the river, about 100m from the road. From Mannings Heath take the A281 towards Horsham and after 1.5km turn into Magpie Lane; just before White's Bridge there is a small layby, with the pillbox in the private woodland on the south side of the road.

To visit the sites in Horsham, it is best to park in one of the town centre car parks. Walk to The Causeway to see the anti-tank pimples, which are marked by a signboard. Horsham Museum is also located in The Causeway. Walk to the end of The Causeway and then through the churchyard. After reaching the river turn right to find the Type 28 pillbox beside a footbridge across the river at Provender Mill. Retrace your steps and continue east along the river, crossing a small footbridge to arrive at the railway bridge at the end of Denne Road where two cylinders are in the river. Turn under the bridge to find the cylinders at the entrance to Denne Park. Retrace your steps, turning right into Chesworth Lane and follow this to its end where the anti-tank pimples can be found at the bridge leading to Chesworth Farm. The Type 28A pillbox is in a private garden in Chesworth Close and cannot be seen. Return to Denne Road and turn right to find the Drill Hall. You can then return to The Causeway via Talbot Lane beside the car park in Denne Road.

Most of the sites to the west of Horsham can be accessed by footpaths. It is best to park at Broadbridge Heath and take the footpath to Broadbridge Heath Farm to see the uprooted anti-tank coffins and adjacent Type 28A pillbox at Mill Bridge, then follow the footpath to High Wood. This is open access land and it is possible to visit the Type 24 pillbox and the coffin at the nearby bridge. It is also possible to see the pillbox at New Bridge and the coffin at Lower Broadbridge Farm by parking in the layby by the garden centre on the Five Oaks Road on the west side of Broadbridge Heath.

Opening times

Horsham Museum is open Monday to Saturday 10am–5pm. Tel: 01403 254959

www.horshammuseum.org

References/Background reading

Burgess, P. & Saunders, A. 1990, *Battle over Sussex 1940*, Midhurst, Middleton Press

Hudson, A. 1986, 'Napoleonic Barracks in Sussex', *Sussex Archaeological Collections* 124, 267–268

Mace, M.F. 1996, *Frontline Sussex: The Defence Lines of West Sussex 1939-1945*, Storrington, Historic Military Press
Martin, R.G. 2005, *Report on ROC 2 Group HQ and UKMO Metropolitan Sector Control*, Denne Road, Horsham, unpublished
White, C. 1995, *When the Siren Sounded*, Worthing, Cliff White Publications
White, C. 1998, *Horsham: The War Years in Pictures*, Horsham, Cliff White Publications

SITE 28: SLINFOLD AND RUDGWICK

Period: **Second World War**
Type of Site: **Pillboxes, Coffins and Defended locality**

History

After passing Horsham, the Corps Stop Line followed the River Arun west to the north of Slinfold and then went on to Bucks Green where there was a defended locality defending the Wanford Bridges. The Stop Line then continued to follow the River Arun to Gibbons Mill at Morgan's Green where the river headed south towards Arundel and the Stop Line continued west into Surrey following the line of the Wey and Arun Canal to Guildford. Along this stretch of the Corps Stop Line pillboxes continued to cover the crossing points over the river, whose sides were cut straight to improve its ability to act as an anti-tank barrier.

At Bucks Green there was a roadblock at Wanford Bridges comprising anti-tank coffins and hairpin rails; concrete blocks were also placed at the sluice gate nearby so that it could not be used to cross the river. The north bank of the river was cut vertically and revetted with timber, while *flame fougasses* comprising steel drums filled with fuel were placed in the banks of the road to the south of the bridge. The bridges were covered by a Type 28 anti-tank pillbox, which was camouflaged as a farm building with a tiled roof and clapboard walls. There was also a spigot mortar nearby, whilst another pillbox was positioned to cover the road from the bridges into Bucks Green village. The village was surrounded by barbed wire entanglements and slit trenches were prepared near the Home Guard HQ which was located in a hut on the village playing field.

The sites today

The first of the pillboxes on the Stop Line near Slinfold is a Type 24 pillbox near Middle Barn (TQ133316) covering a farm bridge over the river. This pillbox is partly sunken and has an external blast wall covering the steps down to its entrance at the rear. At the entrance to Rapkyns Nursing Home on the A281 there is a single anti-tank buoy, with another four white painted buoys at the entrance to Greystones House nearby (TQ 1377 3248). There are further buoys lining the drive to the Nursing Home and at Rapkyns Farm.

57 Type 24 variant pillbox at Dedisham (TQ 1061 3294); note the pre-cast concrete embrasures

58 The Type 24 variant pillbox at Dedisham has an unusual open-topped porch added to its rear with a metal ladder to provide access

About 1km further west is a Type 24 pillbox covering another farm bridge near Rowfold Farm. The pillbox is situated in the middle of a field some 50m north of the river and 100m west of the bridge (TQ 1218 3219), but was originally in a hedgeline. The bridge itself has a concrete block at ground level on its north-west side, which may be the cut-down remains of an anti-tank coffin (TQ 1231 3221).

The river now winds its way north to where it is crossed by the Roman road Stane Street (now the A29). Here a Type 28A anti-tank pillbox is located in the edge of Roman Woods (TQ 1165 3328) facing south to cover the bridge. The pillbox has a 6pdr holdfast and two machine gun embrasures facing south and west. An external brick blast wall has two small embrasures and has been built around a tree, which was presumably left to assist in its camouflage. At Dedisham there is a Type 24 variant pillbox located in a hedgeline (TQ 1061 3294) facing south towards the river (*57*). The pillbox has an unusual brick-built open-topped porch added to its rear with a small embrasure in its north wall. The access into the pillbox is via a metal ladder over the wall of the porch, which is the full height of the pillbox (*58*). Inside the pillbox (which is permanently flooded) there are five pre-cast embrasures with semi-circular concrete tables and a standard blast wall. There are also metal loops on the roof of the pillbox which were presumably for securing its camouflage.

The now disused railway line crosses the River Arun just before reaching Rudgwick and the bridge was blocked with a railblock which has since been removed (TQ 0941 3270). However, a Type 24 pillbox is positioned on the north bank of the river to the south-west of the railway bridge (TQ 0937 3265). The pillbox has an L-shaped external blast wall and is very overgrown. It has a modern locked door and is currently being used as a bat sanctuary.

At Bucks Green most of the fixed defences have been removed by development, works on the river, or during the widening of the road. However, the Type 28 pillbox survives on a large concrete base in a field boundary to the north-east of the bridge (TQ 0843 3274). It has an external blast wall and inside there is a main embrasure with a 6pdr holdfast (*59*) facing south-west, with a machine gun embrasure in the south-east wall behind a blast wall. The brick shuttering has used two different-coloured bricks (*colour plate 20*) and part of the brick shuttering has fallen away due to root damage. A unique square pillbox or machine gun emplacement is located in a garden beside the road from the bridge into Bucks Green (TQ 0826 3275). It has an external brick blast wall covered by two small pistol ports in the rear wall of the pillbox, whilst inside there is a single embrasure facing south towards the bridge.

At Gibbons Mill near Morgan's Green there are two anti-tank coffins blocking a footbridge over a weir to the north-west of Gibbons Mill (TQ 0706 3084) (*60*), whilst a single coffin (probably surviving from two originally) is placed at another small bridge to the west of Gibbons Mill (TQ 0706 3076). There is no evidence for a pillbox covering these bridges, but the mill building is well placed to do this

59 The 6pdr holdfast in the Type 28 pillbox at Bucks Green

and may have been prepared for defence. A possible in-filled loophole can be seen in the west wall of the mill building, which has now been converted to a house.

60 Anti-tank coffins blocking access across the weir at Gibbons Mill (TQ 0706 3084)

Directions and access

The pillbox at Middle Barn can be approached by footpath from the north or south, while the anti-tank buoys are on the south side of the A281 between Broadbridge Heath and Strood Green. The bridge and pillbox at Rowfold Farm are best reached by taking the footpath from Slinfold Church, where limited parking is available. The Type 28 pillbox in Roman Woods is on the edge of the A281 road between the small pump house and the road to Lodge Farm, but there is no parking here. There is no public access to the Type 24 variant pillbox at Dedisham or the Type 24 pillbox near the railway bridge, although there is a footpath (Downs Link) along the disused railway line from the A281.

At Bucks Green it is best to park in the village and walk to Wanford Bridges. The Type 28 pillbox can be seen across the field on the east side of the road just before reaching the bridge, whilst the square pillbox is in the garden of the house adjacent to the road, but is overgrown and difficult to see. There is no public access to either of these pillboxes. The coffins at Gibbons Mill can be reached by a footpath from Morgan's Green; the single coffin can be found by following the footpath west of the mill, whilst the pair of coffins are on the footpath that cuts across the garden on the west side of the mill building.

References/Background reading

PRO WO166/6780 Defences of the defended village of Bucks Green

SITE 29: EAST GRINSTEAD

Period: **Second World War**
Type of Site: **Nodal Point**

History

East Grinstead was designated a Category 'A' Nodal Point and also a Fortress in 1940. Roadblocks were set up at access points into the town, with three sets of anti-tank blocks and four *flame fougasse* sites, one of which was in Dunnings Road where trenches were dug to cover the *flame fougasse* and roadblock, which comprised anti-tank cylinders and buoys. Twelve spigot mortar bases were constructed to cover these sites, together with important road junctions and bridges. The HQ of the 17th Sussex (East Grinstead) Home Guard Battalion was at Sackville College, which was also the HQ of the East Grinstead Nodal Point. A barrier was erected near Sackville College using hairpin rails, whilst a machine gun post was erected to cover the crossroads at the Post Office. An OP was established in the turret on the top of the 80ft-high Playfield Water Tower. In East Sussex, Forest Row sits astride the A22 road on the southern approaches to East Grinstead and was also declared a Nodal Point. There was a roadblock on the A22 beside Kidbrooke Park formed by anti-tank blocks, hairpin rails, anti-tank buoys and a *flame fougasse*. Residents living along the A22 were warned that in the event of an invasion they would be evacuated, as their houses would need to be put into a state of defence.

The East Grinstead civil defence control post was established in Southwick House, whilst the ARP HQ was located at Norton House, with 17 ARP wardens' posts located throughout the town. Public air-raid shelters were located in the existing basements of 15 premises in the centre of the town, whilst surface shelters were constructed in the Vicarage Garden, in Brooklands Way and in West Street. Trench shelters were constructed at the various schools in the town, whilst many houses had their own private shelters.

During the Battle of Britain, the Dorset Arms in East Grinstead was HQ for a London TA searchlight unit stationed on Ashdown Forest. From 1941, 35 Searchlight Regiment RA was deployed across Surrey and Sussex, with three of its batteries spread throughout Sussex. The fourth battery was in Surrey, with the Regimental Headquarters at Ivy House at Lingfield in Surrey just to the north of East Grinstead.

Archibald McIndoe started work at the Queen Victoria Hospital in East Grinstead at the start of the war, having been appointed as the RAF's consultant in plastic surgery. He did pioneering work with pilots who had been horrifically burned in their planes during the Battle of Britain. The pilots who underwent plastic surgery belonged to the Guinea Pig Club and despite their disfigurement and the intensity of their operations, the recovering pilots were incorporated back into society with the help of families in East Grinstead who accepted them into their homes as guests.

61 The trench air-raid shelters at Imberhorne Lower School, previously East Grinstead Grammar School

The site today

Nothing survives of the various roadblocks and other defences that were erected during the Second World War. However Sackville College can be found at the east end of the High Street (TQ 3978 3805) and Playfield Water Tower sits in the corner of a car park at the north end of Church Lane (TQ 3979 3811).

The surface air-raid shelters were all removed after the war, and there are no visible remains of any of the basement shelters, except for the covered stairs that provided access to the basement shelter at Nos 5-9 High Street, which can be seen next to Cubitt & West Estate Agents (TQ 3949 3800). At Imberhorne Lower School (previously East Grinstead Grammar School) there are a number of trench shelters surviving adjacent to the school building (TQ 3855 3915). There are five parallel mounds each 20m long, three of which appear to be connected to form a large 'E' and may therefore be one large trench shelter (*61*), whilst the remaining two may also form a separate shelter, with at least one entrance and two escape hatches visible. A private surface air-raid shelter survives at No. 45 Holtye Road (TQ 3986 3888), although it has subsequently been converted into a shed.

Directions and access

All of the sites within the town centre can be found by parking in one of the car parks and using a town map obtained from the museum. There is no access to the trench shelter at Imberhorne Lower School and it is hidden from view behind the main building. However, the private surface shelter in Holtye Road can be seen from the adjacent pavement.

East Grinstead Museum is situated in Old Market Yard, Cantelupe Road, and is open Wednesday to Saturday 10am-4pm and Sunday and Bank Holidays 2pm-5pm. Tel: 01342 302233

www.eastgrinsteadmuseum.org.uk

References/Background reading

Dobinson, C.S. 2000, 'Searchlight Sites in WWII', *Twentieth Century Fortifications in England*, London, Council for British Archaeology

Griffith, L.A., *From Horse and Cart to Jet Engine*, unpublished notes, East Grinstead Museum Acc. No. 986

Leppard, M.J. 2001, *A History of East Grinstead*, Chichester, Phillimore & Co Ltd

Peters, T.P., *Reminiscences of 1938-1945 by a Head Warden*, East Grinstead, Cullen's. East Grinstead Museum Acc. No. 146

Wood, R.H. 1978, 'Unhappy Far-off Things', *East Grinstead Society Bulletin* 23

4

THE WEST SUSSEX AIRFIELDS

This chapter groups together all of the airfields in West Sussex as they make an interesting collection of sites that are linked together by a common theme.

There were a large number of airfields in West Sussex, especially those grouped around Chichester on the Coastal Plain (*62*). Although one or two had their origins in the First World War, many of them only became operational airfields during the expansion period of the later 1930s. Some of the airfields, such as Tangmere and Westhampnett, were fighter airfields, others were mostly used by Coastal Command or for training. Later in the war, during the build-up towards D-Day, five Advanced Landing Grounds were built, four of which were again in the Chichester area, whilst the fifth (Coolham) was situated to the south of Horsham. These were only operational for a short period of time and by the end of 1944 most had been de-requisitioned and returned to agriculture.

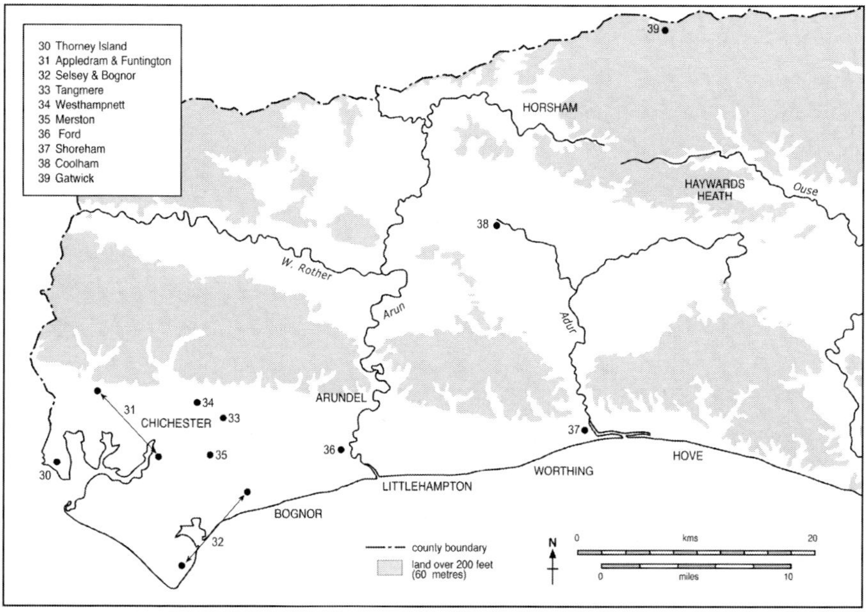

62 Map of West Sussex Airfields

Although some airfields such as Tangmere and Ford continued to be used after the Second World War, both of these and Merston are now disused and are slowly being covered with housing and industrial estates. However, others are still in use; Thorney Island is still a military base and its runway is occasionally used, Westhampnett is now a private airfield, whilst Shoreham is a lively small airport and Gatwick has grown into one of the busiest airports in the world.

SITE 30: THORNEY ISLAND

Period: **Second World War**
Type of site: **Airfield**

History

Construction of an airfield at Thorney Island began at the end of 1935, when the site began to be cleared. Over the next two years barrack blocks, administrative buildings and workshops were built; together with six Type C Hangars, surrounded by concrete hardstandings. The airfield was officially opened on 3 February 1938 as part of No. 16 Group, Coastal Command and the Wildebeestes of Nos 22 and 42 Squadrons were flown in. In 1940 the airfield was expanded to take over almost all of Thorney Island and Beauforts arrived to replace the Wildebeestes. Ansons of No. 48 Squadron and No. 1 Coastal Artillery Co-operation Unit were also based at Thorney Island.

Although there had been a few minor attacks by the Luftwaffe in early August 1940, a force of 28 Ju87 Stukas attempted to attack the airfield on the 18 August and although the attack was broken up, two of the hangars were badly damaged and three aircraft on the ground were destroyed, whilst a fuel dump and air-raid shelter were also hit. As a result of this and later raids, an airfield K/Q decoy site (No. 52) was set up at West Wittering and became one of the most successful in terms of the number of Luftwaffe attacks it attracted until its closure in June 1942 (see Site 1). Given its vulnerable position on the coast, the defences for Thorney Island were concentrated around the edges and comprised numerous pillboxes and gun emplacements equipped with 27 machine guns and one 75mm field gun, whilst the local anti-aircraft defences included five searchlights and three 40mm Bofors. The grass runways were camouflaged by painted hedges to give the impression that there was a patchwork of small fields across the island.

In 1942 three concrete runways and a perimeter track were built, while 17 Extra Oversize Blister hangars were dispersed around the airfield. Throughout 1942 and 1943, numerous Coastal Command squadrons were based at Thorney Island flying a variety of aircraft including Hampdens, Hudsons and Blenheims on anti-shipping strikes and anti-submarine patrols. However, in early 1944 the Coastal Command squadrons had left, and Nos 123 and 136 Airfields flying Typhoons were established at Thorney Island. After D-day these squadrons moved to France, and were replaced by Mosquito FBVI's of No. 140 Wing, until they too moved to France in February 1945.

In 1946 the airfield was once again used by Mosquitos and Beaufighters of Coastal Command, until it was transferred to Fighter Command at the end of 1947. Meteors and Spitfires were based at Thorney Island until May 1950, when the airfield was transferred to Flying Training Command. In 1962 the airfield was once again transferred, this time to No. 38 Group Transport Command who used it until 1975. When they left, a flight of SAR Whirlwind helicopters of the No. 22 Squadron were the sole occupants, until these too moved out in January 1976 and the airfield was then closed. Used for two years as a refugee camp, the airfield was finally turned into an army base in 1984.

The site today

Thorney Island is currently the base for 47 Regiment Royal Artillery and has been much refurbished and modified. Although many of the original airfield buildings, such as the control tower, have been removed, there are still a number remaining including four of the Type C Hangars (SU759029), the barrack blocks and some of the administration buildings. On the west side of the airfield, the ammunition storage compound surrounded by earthen banks (SU749034) lies abandoned and overgrown. The runways and much of the original concrete perimeter track and dispersals are also still extant and some of the perimeter defences around the coast also survive. The seawall was built in the 1930s and modified as an anti-tank wall in 1940-41 by adding reinforced concrete to form a steeper outer face. Sections of the wall survive at SU 7655 0416, SU 7688 0098 and SU 7510 0460.

At the north end of the island facing towards the bridge over Great Deep, there is a brick-shuttered Type 22 pillbox (SU 7533 0376) with an internal Y-shaped blast wall. There may have also been a gun emplacement located nearby covering the bridge, but there is no trace of this today. Along the west side of the island there are a number of pillboxes and machine gun emplacements. The first is a corrugated iron-shuttered Type 23 pillbox, facing west towards the coast with its open anti-aircraft enclosure on the east side (SU 7486 0304). The roof is covered with turf, which may be part of its original camouflage. A little further south there was a rectangular machine gun emplacement, which was constructed from pre-cast concrete blocks with a corrugated iron roof (SU 7500 0287); unfortunately this was demolished in the late 1990s. Sitting in the edge of a small plantation is a small square open-topped brick emplacement, perhaps for an anti-aircraft machine gun, with an entrance in its south side protected by an external blast wall (SU 7506 0264). In the south-west corner of the island, close to some surviving dispersals, is a square brick-walled emplacement for a Bofors anti-aircraft gun (SU 7492 0224). It has a concrete floor, with ammunition locker bays in two corners and a protected entrance on its north side.

Along the south coast of the island most of the installations have been lost to coastal erosion; those recently lost include two Type 22 pillboxes at SU 7622 0122

63 Circular brick weapons pit on the east coast of Thorney Island. *Image by Jo Short for Chichester Harbour Conservancy*

and SU 7667 0113, and a Type 23 pillbox at SU757019. There is a surviving small square open-topped brick emplacement, perhaps for an anti-aircraft machine gun, with an entrance in its east side at SU 7652 0110, near Longmere Point. This emplacement has a new wooden roof and is currently used as a bird hide. Most of the possible anti-tank cubes along the south coast of Thorney Island have also been lost to coastal erosion.

Along the east coast, south of Stanbury Point, at SU 7700 0260 there is a small filled-in circular brick-built weapons pit 1.4m in diameter. A second circular brick-built weapons pit (*63*) at SU 7694 0285 is 2.5m in diameter, and is positioned up against the inner edge of the seawall. It has a holdfast in the centre of its concrete base and was probably for an anti-aircraft weapon or searchlight. North of Stanbury Point is an overgrown corrugated iron-shuttered Type 23 pillbox (SU 7679 0329) with the open anti-aircraft enclosure on its east side. A little further north is a three-sided brick rectangular infantry section post (SU 7688 0298) built into the embankment and facing east.

Directions and access

As the airfield site at Thorney Island is an army camp, there is no access onto the airfield itself. There is a coastal footpath around the outside of the island, access to which is controlled by the army. It is best to park near Emsworth or Southbourne, which are on the A259, and follow the footpaths south to Thorney Island. At the gated entrance to the footpath you are required to report in and at the end of your walk, check out. The surviving positions along the east and south sides of the island are visible from the footpath, but those on the west coast are within the army camp and cannot be seen.

References/Background reading

Ashworth, R.C.B. 1985, *Action Stations 9. Military airfields of the Central South and South-East*, Wellingborough, Patrick Stephens Ltd

Brooks, R.J. 1993, *Sussex Airfields in the Second World War*, Newbury, Countryside Books

Price, A. 1990, *The Hardest Day*, London, Arrow Books

Thorney Island: Plan of proposed layout 1160/35/17 dated 1935 (RAF Museum)

SITE 31: APPLEDRAM AND FUNTINGTON

Period: **Second World War**
Type of site: **Advanced Landing Grounds**

History

Construction of the ALG at Appledram commenced in February 1943 and was completed by the end of May. Two Summerfield track runways were laid out in a crucifix on the flat grassland and the personnel were accommodated in tents. Four Blister Hangars were erected in 1944 and metalled hardstandings were also provided at the same time, whilst some farm cottages were taken over as additional accommodation and a bomb dump was established near the Black Horse pub.

The Typhoons of the No. 124 Airfield arrived shortly after the ALG was ready in May 1943 and were soon operating over occupied France until July when they left and the ALG reverted to the status of Care and Maintenance. No. 134 Airfield, comprising Czech pilots with Spitfire IXs, arrived in April 1944 and operated from Appledram until replaced by the Poles of 131 Wing later in June. 2804 Squadron RAF Regiment was deployed to protect the airfield with its eight 40mm Bofors and eight 20mm Hispano guns in April 1944. The Poles left on 16 July and the ALG was de-requisitioned on 6 November.

Funtington was originally selected as an emergency landing ground or overflow for the neighbouring airfields in the Chichester area in 1942 and was then upgraded to an ALG in February 1943. Two Sommerfield Track runways were laid out initially and then at the end of 1943 it was upgraded with concrete taxiways and hardstandings, and four Blister Hangars.

The first aircraft to use the ALG were the Mustang Is of No. 130 Airfield in September 1943, who stayed just a few weeks. No. 143 Airfield arrived with

Typhoons in April 1944, again staying just a few weeks before moving to Hurn, to be replaced by No. 144 Airfield with Spitfire IXs. A number of other Wings used Funtingdon in quick succession during the time of the D-Day landings, with No. 132 Wing being the last before the departure to France in August 1944.

The airfield was de-requisitioned in December 1944 and was quickly cleared, although the Blister hangers were retained for storage for a few months longer, before finally being removed as well.

The sites today

Virtually nothing remains to be seen today of either ALG, apart from gaps in hedgerows where the runways were located. There are also some tracks that appear to follow the lines of the perimeter track of Funtingdon ALG at the research establishment on the north side of Common Road and a track that runs north from this road to Racton Park Farm.

Directions and access

Appledram ALG was situated at SU839018, with the north-south runway on the west side of the A286 between Chichester Harbour Marina and Apuldram. Funtingdon ALG was at SU790085 with its east-west runway broadly following the line of Common Road.

References/Background reading

Ashworth, R.C.B. 1985, *Action Stations 9. Military airfields of the Central South and South-East*, Wellingborough, Patrick Stephens Ltd

Brooks, R.J. 1993, *Sussex Airfields in the Second World War*, Newbury, Countryside Books

Rimell, K. 1992, *Merlin and the Sabre (Story of RAF Apuldram 1943-5)*, Wittering, Castle Printers

SITE 32: SELSEY AND BOGNOR

Period: **Second World War**
Type of site: **Advanced Landing Grounds**

History

In 1942 an area of land (SZ865955) to the west of Church Norton (see Site 2) that had previously been a private airfield in the 1930s, was requisitioned and in 1943 an ALG known as RAF Selsey was constructed. Some local buildings were used for accommodation and Norton Priory was used as the HQ. In late 1943, additional facilities in the form of four Blister hangars were added to supplement an existing civil hangar that had been requisitioned and PSP tracking and hard standing was laid around the ALG. It was initially used by Spitfire Vs and Typhoons of No. 121

Airfield and later squadrons of Spitfire IXs from No. 135 Wing were based on the ALG during D-Day and for a short period afterwards. After the war, the hangers and buildings were removed and the site reverted to agriculture.

An ALG was established at Bognor in early 1943 with two Summerfield Track runways laid out and tented accommodation for the personnel. The HQ and offices were located at Morells Farm and the petrol installation was on the west side of the B2166, which was closed as it was crossed by one of the runways. Later in 1943, four Blister Hangars were constructed, with taxiways and hardstandings also being provided. The ALG opened on the 1 June 1943 and was immediately occupied by No. 122 Airfield with Spitfire VBs. After a month, No. 122 Airfield left and the ALG was deserted until No. 132 Airfield arrived in March 1944 with Spitfire IXs. They left on 21 June and were replaced by No. 83 Group Support Unit, which held stocks of reserve aircraft and replacement pilots, and No. 1310 Flight with ambulance Ansons. These units finally left the Bognor ALG in September 1944.

The sites today

On the road from the B2145 to Church Norton is a plaque on a concrete plinth commemorating RAF Selsey (SZ 8661 9532). Nothing else of the ALG can be seen today, although when standing at the plaque, the flat nature of the ground on which the ALG was situated can clearly be seen.

The Bognor ALG was decommissioned at the end of 1944, with the site being handed back to its owners in early 1945. There is little evidence of the ALG surviving at the site today, as all of the matting, the hardstandings, taxiways and the hangars were removed at the end of the war. On Chalcraft Lane there is a large section of hedge missing close to the cemetery where the runway crossed this road, which was also closed. Morells Farm (SU 9082 0042) is on the B2166 and, just south of there, Old Chapel Forge was used as the paymaster's office (SU 9085 0010).

Directions and access

The Selsey ALG was situated at SU865957 between the B2145 and the minor road to Church Norton. The Bognor ALG was located at SU915005 between the B2166 and Chalcraft Lane. Both sites are now farmland with limited footpath access.

References/Background reading

Ashworth, R.C.B. 1985, *Action Stations 9. Military airfields of the Central South and South-East*, Wellingborough, Patrick Stephens Ltd

Brooks, R.J. 1993, *Sussex Airfields in the Second World War*, Newbury, Countryside Books

Endacott, S. 2005, *It Started with a Map: The story of the Bognor Regis Advanced Landing Ground 1943-1944*, Littlehampton, Burchell Design & Print

Bognor: Lay-Out 616/44 dated Nov 1943 (RAF Museum)

SITE 33: TANGMERE AIRFIELD

Period: **First World War to Cold War**
Type of site: **Airfield**

History

Tangmere originated as a training aerodrome during 1917 and was provided with seven GS Belfast Truss hangars, a large Handley Page shed and wooden hut accommodation. After a short period of use by the USAAS in 1918, the airfield was used for training and as a holding station for RAF squadrons returning from France. It was closed in 1918 and was then used for storage, until reactivated in 1926. The airfield was subsequently used as a fighter station with Nos 1 and 43 Squadrons equipped with Siskin IIIAs. The station was enhanced by the construction of permanent brick barrack blocks, married quarters, station sick quarters, an airmen's dining hall and a NAAFI canteen in 1926, whilst three of the hangars and the Handley Page shed were retained.

During the expansion period, further squadrons were established and new barrack blocks, workshops and MT buildings were constructed, whilst the runway was extended. At the start of the Battle of Britain, Tangmere had three squadrons of Hurricanes (43, 145 and 601 Squadrons) which were joined by other squadrons during the following months. On 16 August 1940, Tangmere was heavily attacked by Stukas, which destroyed three hangars and damaged others, whilst numerous other buildings were wrecked. As a result of this raid, the Sector Operations Room, which had been based at Tangmere, moved to St James' School in Chichester.

As the war progressed, other units began using Tangmere. The Fighter Interception Unit with Blenheims and then Beaufighters, No. 1455 Flight with Havocs equipped with searchlights for night interceptions and the clandestine Lysanders of the No. 161 Squadron all used the airfield between 1940 and 1941. From 1942 through to the end of the war, Spitfires and Typhoons used the airfield until they all departed for the continent and in 1945 the Central Fighter Establishment was set up.

Later in 1945, three new T2 hangars (*64*) were built on the foundations of the bombed hangars and many temporary wartime buildings were removed. Tangmere then became a base for Meteors, with Nos 1 and 43 Squadrons returning to the base until 1950 when the No. 43 Squadron was replaced by the No. 29 Squadron flying Meteor night fighter aircraft. In 1955 No. 34 Squadron joined No. 1 Squadron, both flying Hunter Mk 5 aircraft, and then in 1958, No. 90 (Signals) Group replaced them. The airfield was then part of No. 38 Group of Transport Command until 1970 when it was reduced to Care and Maintenance status. Since then the three T2 hangars have been used for food storage and parts of the airfield have been taken over for industrial use, or covered by large greenhouses.

64 One of the three T2 Hangars surviving at Tangmere

The sites today

Although under continuing threat from development, there are numerous parts of the airfield that can be seen today. The Tangmere Military Aviation Museum opened in 1982 in one of the airfield buildings and has expanded into a thriving little museum today (SU 9058 0607). There are a number of aircraft on display outside, together with a Pickett-Hamilton turret (from Merston airfield – Site 35), whilst the exhibits inside cover the history of the airfield.

At the northern end of the airfield there are large areas of concrete hardstanding and perimeter road, together with the three T2 hangars (SU 9060 0638 to SU 9092 0641), the fire station and a large shed. Nearby the Control Tower (*colour plate 21*) stands derelict and boarded up (SU 9109 0640). Hidden between the housing development and industrial estate are a number of administrative buildings (SU 9083 0665); including an accommodation building, the MT section garages and workshops, NAAFI building and a transformer building.

Along East Hampnett Lane, on the north-east side of the airfield, is a bulk fuel installation site (SU 9176 0672), now used as a waste water treatment works. At least one semi-sunken bulk fuel bunker can be seen, together with a Nissen hut and, close to the entrance, a small office building. At the Easthampnett Caravan Park there is a guardhouse, hut bases and a small building (SU 9205 0687), all part of a dispersed site for RAF Tangmere.

On the south-east corner of the airfield there are further sections of hardstanding and perimeter track, together with three pairs of post-war fighter dispersal blast pens (SU 9183 0557, SU 9182 0567 and SU 9179 0578). Each blast pen comprises a parallel pair of wood-shuttered concrete blast walls, which taper

65 Two of the post-war fighter dispersal blast pens at Tangmere, which are now used for compost storage

towards the top, sitting on an area of concrete hardstanding (65). At least one blast pen also has a rear wall of concrete panels retained by an earthen bank. Two blast pens have stencilled serial numbers ('15' and '16') on their blast walls and Pen '15' has a rectangular concrete building base on its east side.

Directions and access

Follow the signs to Tangmere Military Aviation Museum from the roundabout on the A27. Having visited the museum, return towards the A27, but turn into Churchwood Drive. Follow this to the end turning right into Fulmar Way. Park here and cross the barrier at the end of the road to see the Control Tower and then turn right to see the T2 hangars and fire station, although these are behind a security fence. Turn back into Churchwood Drive and then right into City Fields Way. Park at the gate to see the other administrative buildings, although these may be lost to development in the near future and there is no access to them.

From the A27 turn into Nyton Road (B2233), then into East Hampnett Lane. The caravan park is immediately on the right and the bulk fuel installation a further 500m along the lane on the left. To find the blast pens, return to the B2233, then turn right to Aldingbourne (signposted Oving); after 500m turn right to Aldingbourne village and follow the lane past Aldinge Farm. Park at the end and follow the footpath onto the airfield perimeter track where the blast pens can be seen in front of you. The site is currently an Environment Agency waste disposal site and the blast pens are used for storing compost. Permission to visit the site can be obtained from the site office, but a hard hat is required to gain access to the site.

Opening times

Tangmere Military Aviation Museum is open February and November 10am-4.30pm, March to end of October 10am-5.30pm. Tel. 01243 790090

www.tangmere-museum.org.uk

References/Background reading

Ashworth, R.C.B. 1985, *Action Stations 9. Military airfields of the Central South and South-East*, Wellingborough, Patrick Stephens Ltd

Brooks, R.J. 1993, *Sussex Airfields in the Second World War*, Newbury, Countryside Books

Saunders, A. 1992, *RAF Tangmere in Old Photographs*, Stroud, Sutton Publishing Ltd

Saunders, A. 1998, *RAF Tangmere Revisited*, Stroud, Sutton Publishing Ltd

2007, *A Brief History of RAF Tangmere*, Tangmere Military Aviation Museum

Tangmere Location Plan 2322/27 dated Dec. 1927 (RAF Museum)

Tangmere Site Plan – First Contract (1935) 233/35 (RAF Museum)

Tangmere Site Plan – Second Contract 4173/35/14 (RAF Museum)

SITE 34: WESTHAMPNETT AIRFIELD

Period: **Second World War**

Type of site: **Airfield**

History

The land at Goodwood Estate was requisitioned in 1938 for use as an Emergency Landing Ground (ELG) for RAF Tangmere. However, after the fall of France in May 1940, it was upgraded to a satellite airfield for Tangmere with four grass runways laid out using Sommerfield Tracking, together with a number of Blister hangars and a watch office. The officers were accommodated in nearby Shopwyke Hall, whilst the airmen were accommodated under canvas. No. 145 Squadron with hurricanes was the first to use Westhampnett, later being replaced by No. 602 Squadron with Spitfires.

Waterlogging was a continual problem during the winter of 1940/1, so a concrete perimeter track and hardstanding dispersals were built in early 1941, whilst additional Blister hangars were built and Nissen huts provided upgraded accommodation. A large communal site was established at Westerton and other dispersed sites were located around the airfield. The ground defences for the airfield included seven gun posts (pillboxes), distributed around the perimeter of the airfield and the Battle HQ was located on the northern perimeter. During 1941 and into 1942 the airfield was used by a variety of squadrons and in July 1942 became USAAF Base 352 for a few months, hosting the 31 Fighter Group.

Returning to RAF control, Westhampnett was used by a number of Spitfire and Typhoon squadrons through until after D-Day when the squadrons redeployed to the continent and the airfield was placed into Care and Maintenance in early 1945.

The Naval Air Fighting Development Unit moved into Westhampnett in July 1945, but had moved out in November the same year, with the airfield once again being placed into Care and Maintenance and finally closed as a military airfield in May 1946.

Many of the airfield buildings were removed after the war and the airfield was opened as the Goodwood Motor Racing Circuit using the airfield perimeter track in 1948. Although no longer used for competitive racing, the circuit is still used for recreational activities today, whilst the centre of the track is used as a runway for the small airfield that opened in 1958.

The sites today

A number of the wartime administration buildings are still in use today, whilst others survive around the perimeter of the airfield. However, many of the perimeter buildings have been removed or buried during the construction of the embankment that now surrounds the airfield. As you pass through the entrance to the airfield, the long single-storey building on the right of the entrance was the Gas Clothing and Respirator Store (SU 8796 0748). Turning left you pass the Parachute Store (*colour plate 22*), now used as a shop (SU 8795 0742), and a short distance behind this is a small Drying Room and Latrine building (SU 8793 0740). Crossing the car park, there is a toilet block on the right, which may have originally been the W.A.A.F. Latrine (SU 8792 0734); sitting beside it is a blast wall. On the far side of the car park is a 1941 USAAF Pattern Perimeter Control Tower (*66*), now used as a café (SU 8791 0727). Returning towards the entrance there is a rectangular brick structure alongside the main road adjacent to a small car park, which was a Transformer Enclosure (SU 8798 0738). Cross over the entrance road to the two large Nissen huts (*67*), which were the main workshops (SU 8794 0753) and on their west side the roof and stairway to a below-ground air-raid shelter can be seen (SU 8793 0750); this is still in use today and has a structure added to its north end.

Two further buildings exist in the north-east corner of the airfield. At the closed gate there is a large windowless brick building with two external blast walls protecting the entrances in the south and east walls (SU 8798 0774), which was the airfield's Electricity Sub-station. Nearby is a long single-story building (SU 8795 0778) which was the Squadron Office. On the northern perimeter is a long single-story Maycrete building, which was a latrine and Drying room (SU 8749 0788). This is very overgrown, but still has its internal fixtures and fittings, and may have been used as a latrine block after the war. The Battle HQ was adjacent to this building, but no trace of this now survives. A short distance further on is one of two surviving gun posts. It comprises a two-story circular pillbox, now covered with ivy

66 The 1941 USAAF Pattern Perimeter Control Tower at Westhampnett Airfield has been renovated and is currently used as a café

67 These two large Nissen huts at Westhampnett Airfield were the Main Workshops for the wartime airfield, and are still used as workshops today

68 The three-story Quadrant Tower is located near the western perimeter track at Westhampnett Airfield, and is a strange facility to find on a fighter airfield

and situated adjacent to the northern perimeter fence (SU 8743 0791). It appears to be identical to the second pillbox, which is described in more detail below.

Along the west side of the perimeter there is an air-raid shelter (SU 8680 0773) located outside the current perimeter fence. This is brick built with a concrete roof and is partly below ground. There is an entrance at each end with a protective blast wall. A little further south is another Transformer Enclosure (SU

8691 0760). The blast wall is built with grey bricks and inside there are some of its internal fittings still present. There is an unusual three-story Quadrant Tower, built of brick, with a concrete roof, located near the western perimeter track (SU 8701 0753). It has a door at ground level and windows in the upper two storeys (*68*), while the stairs at the rear appear to be more recent additions. A Quadrant Tower was intended for bombing practice and is thus a strange facility on a fighter airfield. However, it does not appear on the 1945 map of the airfield and may be associated with the post-war use of the airfield by the Naval Air Fighting Development Unit. The final installation around the perimeter of the airfield is the second two-storey circular pillbox (SU 8725 0689). It is brick shuttered and has an entrance on its north side, which is below ground level. There are six pre-cast concrete embrasures on the lower storey, which are at ground level, and a further six embrasures on the second storey (*69*). On its east side there is a large concrete pipe inserted into the ground, which may have been an anti-aircraft machine gun position.

The 1945 map of the airfield does not show any buildings within the perimeter track, however, today there are a number of buildings which may have been erected during the latter part of the war or immediately post-war, in the central part of the airfield. On the north side of the airfield and outside the perimeter, is a Type T1 hangar (SU 8781 0797).

69 This two-storey circular pillbox is located on the western side of Westhampnett Airfield (SU 8725 0689). It has six pre-cast concrete embrasures on the lower storey and a further six embrasures on the second storey.

Little survives of the communal sites or other dispersed sites that were located around the airfield. The main communal site was at Westerton and here some of the concrete roads survive in Richmond Road (SU885074), which was the sick quarters site, and elsewhere in the village. Along one concrete road, on the east side of the village, there is an air-raid shelter in a field (SU 8887 0747) together with sections of concrete road and building bases. The shelter is above ground, but covered with an earth mound and has two opposing entrances in the centre, with internal blast walls that have been removed and a circular vent at each end. Concrete roads and building bases can be seen at the sites of some of the other dispersed sites; for example at Communal Site 2 (SU 8855 0772) and Dispersed Site 2 (SU 8910 0810).

Directions and access

Westhampnett airfield is on the north-east side of Chichester and is signposted (as Goodwood Aerodrome) from the roundabout on the A27. Access to the car park, café and adjacent buildings is possible, but there is no access to the sites around the perimeter or to the interior of the airfield without permission. A footpath can be followed around the western side of the perimeter from the Lavant Straight, which takes you past the air-raid shelter, which is outside the airfield fence, and on the right side of the path. The Transformer Enclosure, Quadrant Tower and pillbox can also be seen from this footpath. The T1 hangar can be seen on the north side of the Lavant Straight and the air-raid shelter at Westerton can be seen from the adjacent concrete road, although both sites are on private property.

References/Background reading

Ashworth, R.C.B. 1985, *Action Stations 9. Military airfields of the Central South and South-East*, Wellingborough, Patrick Stephens Ltd

Brooks, R.J. 1993, *Sussex Airfields in the Second World War*, Newbury, Countryside Books

Delve, K. 2005, *The Military Airfields of Britain: Southern England*, Marlborough, Crowood Press Ltd

2007, *A Brief History of RAF Tangmere*, Tangmere Military Aviation Museum

Westhampnett Airfield Site Plan 4594/45 dated May 1945 (RAF Museum)

SITE 35: MERSTON AIRFIELD

Period: **Second World War**
Type of Site: **Airfield**

History

The land at Merston, just two miles south-west of RAF Tangmere, was requisitioned in 1939 with the intention of using it as a 'K' airfield decoy site, but it was then established as a satellite of Tangmere in 1940. The grass runways became very waterlogged and it was not until Spring 1941 that the airfield was finally operational. The airfield was encircled by a concrete perimeter track, while the domestic site was located near Marsh Farm and the technical site was near the nurseries on the west side of the airfield. Six Blister hangars and some blast pens were also added. No. 145 Squadron operating Spitfires was the first squadron to use Merston, followed by a number of other squadrons until August 1942, when a squadron of the USAAF 31 Fighter Group moved in. Over the winter of 1942/3 two Sommerfield Track runways were laid, along with 20 hardstandings, whilst additional accommodation was added to take the increase in personnel. When Merston reopened in May 1943, a number of squadrons used the airfield in quick succession, before No.124 Airfield arrived in October 1943 with its Typhoons. These were followed by other units, until the Spitfires of No.142 Wing became the last flying unit to operate from Merston, leaving in August 1944.

The airfield was reduced to Care and Maintenance soon after this and the Sommerfield Track was quickly removed. In March 1945 the airfield was used by an Air Disarmament Unit and in November 1945 the buildings were handed over to the Admiralty and used for storage.

The sites today

The site of the airfield is now largely covered with greenhouses, but almost the entire perimeter track still exists, with a good section that can be seen from the footpath at SU 8871 0342 (*70*). There is a transformer building at Marsh Farm (SU 8875 0261), which was part of the domestic site, together with a good section of

70 Part of the perimeter track on the east side of Merston Airfield (SU 8871 0342)

perimeter track. At the technical site there is a single-storey brick hut (approx. SU 8808 0354) together with another transformer building and there may be other structures hidden amongst the agricultural buildings at Vinnetrow Farm. On the north-east side of the airfield there is an overgrown 32-man sleeping shelter (SU 8873 0352) and on a dispersed site near Downlands Farm there is a BCF hut (approx. SU 8871 0342).

Also surviving at Merston is the airfield's Battle Headquarters (approx. SU891027), which is the only surviving example in Sussex. This partly buried concrete structure was built to a standard design (11008/41) and was intended as the command post for the airfield's ground defences in the event of an attack. It has a set of entrance steps, protected by concrete blast walls, down into the interior, which is divided into a number of rooms. Projecting above ground is the domed observation cupola, with a narrow observation slit giving a 360° field of vision across the airfield. Interestingly, the Pickett-Hamilton turret on display at Tangmere Military Aviation Museum (Site 33) apparently originated from Merston airfield and was found by REs when clearing the airfield of pipe-mines.

Directions and access

Merston airfield is situated on the south-east side of Chichester and is best approached along the minor road to Runcton from the A27/A259 roundabout. This takes you past the technical site at Vinnetrow Farm and then into Runcton. Turn left at the roundabout, then take the minor road on the left to Merston which takes you past the domestic site at Marsh Farm, and then past the site of the Battle HQ, although all of these sites are on private land and cannot be visited. On reaching the A259, turn left, take the B2144 north at the roundabout and pull into the layby on the left. The BCF hut can be seen on the far side of the field on the east side of the road. Return to the roundabout and take the A259 to Chichester, then turn off after 0.75km and park near the Kings Head public house. From here, take the footpath to the south-west which will take you past the 32-man sleeping shelter and onto the airfield perimeter track. The footpaths can then be followed to other parts of the airfield.

References/Background reading

Ashworth, R.C.B. 1985, *Action Stations 9. Military airfields of the Central South and South-East*, Wellingborough, Patrick Stephens Ltd

Delve, K. 2005, *The Military Airfields of Britain: Southern England*, Marlborough, Crowood Press Ltd

Mace, M.F. 1997, *Sussex Wartime Relics and Memorials*, Storrington, Historic Military Press.

2007, *A Brief History of RAF Tangmere*, Tangmere Military Aviation Museum

www.atlantikwall.co.uk/atlantikwall/atlantikwall_html/home_page_html/home_page.shtml

SITE 36: FORD AIRFIELD

Period: **First and Second World Wars**
Type of Site: **Airfield**

History

The aerodrome at Ford Junction (also known as Yapton) was authorised in 1917 and work commenced at the site in 1918. The technical site was situated on the west side of the aerodrome and comprised six hangars and a large aircraft-repair shed. The first aircraft to use the aerodrome were FE 2Bs of No. 148 Squadron RFC in March, before the aerodrome was handed over to the USAAS as a Training Field. However, the war ended before any training was completed and the Americans moved out, with Ford then being used as a demobilisation centre, until its closure in 1920.

Flying restarted at Ford in 1930, when it was used by a number of commercial organisations, including the Ford Motor Company and then Flight Refuelling Ltd for the development of refuelling trials. The Air Ministry re-acquired the airfield in 1937 and it was used as a School of Naval Cooperation by No. 17 (Training) Group of RAF Coastal Command, with a wooden hutted camp and five Bellman Hangars being built. In 1939 it was transferred to the Admiralty and commissioned as HMS Peregrine, with the training unit renamed the RN Observer School.

The airfield was attacked by 28 JU87 Stukas on 18 August 1940, destroying two hangars, numerous stores and accommodation huts, together with 17 aircraft, whilst 28 people were killed and 75 wounded. As a result of this attack HMS Peregrine was closed and Ford was transferred to No. 11 Group RAF Fighter Command, with Blenheims and Beaufighters of the Fighter Interception Unit (FIU) arriving in December 1940. The airfield's facilities were enhanced with two tarmac runways and taxiways being constructed, together with some blast pens, whilst some Blister hangars were distributed around the perimeter track. The FIU continued to operate from Ford with increasing success until April 1944 when it moved to Wittering, to be replaced by the Mustangs of No. 122 Airfield. For the D-Day operations Nos 125 and 144 Wings were operating from Ford and as these moved to France, they were replaced by other units until they had all moved on to the continent. In September the FIU returned to Ford and continued to operate from the airfield as part of the Night Fighter Development Wing until early 1945 when it transferred to Tangmere.

In July 1945, Ford was transferred back to the Admiralty and recommissioned as HMS Peregrine, with numerous squadrons moving to the airfield over the following year. In 1948 the airfield was closed for refurbishment, with the runways and taxiways being resurfaced; three new hangars were erected and the technical and much of the domestic area was rebuilt. It re-opened in March 1950 with the two based units being 703 Squadron (as the Service Trials Unit) and 771

Squadron (as the Fleet Requirements Unit), whilst front-line squadrons used the airfield whilst working-up prior to joining their aircraft carriers. Although some rebuilding started in 1956, this was halted as the result of the reductions in defence spending announced in 1958 and by September of that year flying had ceased at Ford, with the airfield being paid off in November the same year.

Many of the airfield buildings, such as the control tower and Bellman hangars, were demolished, but others survive, either as part of Ford Open Prison or because they were incorporated into the industrial parks that have sprung up around the airfield.

The sites today

Much of the domestic site has been retained due to its incorporation into Ford Open Prison, where many of the original buildings are still used. On the west side of Ford Road numerous wooden huts, Maycrete buildings and brick buildings can be seen, together with at least one Nissen hut. Around the car park of the prison are a guard post, transformer building and a number of small buildings with armoured doors (TQ001028). The main runways survive almost intact within the central part of the airfield, although some industrial buildings are now covering parts of them.

Along Ford Lane there are surviving parts of the technical site. At Ford Lane Business Park (SU 9950 0385) there are some Maycrete buildings, together with around 60 anti-tank cylinders (*71*), whilst some other buildings, including a Nissen hut are situated around Wicks Farm (SU 9938 0386). To the south of Ford Lane there are two B1 Hangars that are currently used by Tarmac (SU 9945 0341), whilst further on there is an unusual large building that has recently been renovated together with a generator hut (SU 9881 0393). On the west side of the airfield there may be some surviving buildings in the Ford Airfield Industrial Estate (SU990031), but recent development appears to have removed most of these. Three Stanton air-raid shelters survived adjacent to Yapton Road (B2233) at SU987027, however it has not been possible to confirm whether they are still present. A private air-raid shelter also exists in a garden in Yapton (SU974033). North of Horsemere Green Lane at SU 9949 0236 is a surviving Blister Hangar (*colour plate 23*).

Directions and access

Many of the surviving buildings at Ford can be seen by driving around the four roads that surround the airfield, although most of the sites are on private land with no public access. The buildings at Ford Open Prison can be seen from Ford Road and the Prison car park, but note that photography is not permitted here. Parts of the central airfield area, including the runways, can be reached when the regular Ford Airfield Market and car boot sales are held.

References/Background reading

Ashworth, R.C.B. 1985, *Action Stations 9. Military airfields of the Central South and South-East*, Wellingborough, Patrick Stephens Ltd

71 Maycrete building at Ford Lane Business Park, together with some of the 60 anti-tank cylinders at this site

Brooks, R.J. 1993, *Sussex Airfields in the Second World War*, Newbury, Countryside Books

Delve, K. 2005, *The Military Airfields of Britain: Southern England*, Marlborough, Crowood Press Ltd

Mace, M.F. 1997, *Sussex Wartime Relics and Memorials*, Storrington, Historic Military Press

Price, A. 1990, *The Hardest Day*, London, Arrow Books

www.atlantikwall.co.uk/atlantikwall/atlantikwall_html/home_page_html/home_page.shtml

SITE 37: SHOREHAM AIRFIELD

Period: **First and Second World Wars**
Type of site: **Airfield**

History

Shoreham was first established as an aerodrome in early 1911 with a 2000ft grass runway and by its official opening as Shoreham (Brighton) Aerodrome in June 1911 it had 10 wooden hangars. The aerodrome was requisitioned in 1914 and became a training establishment for the RFCs with No. 3 Training Squadron in residence using Farmans, FE2s and Avro 504s. During the war additional hangars and other buildings were erected. From 1919 the airfield was used by the emerging Canadian Air Force, which was disbanded in 1920 and its aircraft crated and shipped to Canada in December 1921. The airfield was then closed, its land reverting to cattle grazing.

In the early 1930s interest in a local municipal airport grew again and by 1934 work had started on a new Terminal Building and a new double hangar and workshops. Shoreham Airport opened in 1936 with a two-day air display and scheduled flights were started to destinations in France, Jersey and elsewhere in Britain. In 1937 the Martin School of Air Navigation was set up at Shoreham to train RAF Volunteer Reserve personnel under contract to the Air Ministry, and later became No. 16 Elementary and Reserve Flying Training School. At the outbreak of war, the training school moved away and for a short while Shoreham become a thriving international airport until the fall of European countries and Italy's entry into the war led to the suspension of the routes. Due to its location adjacent to the River Adur, the airfield's defences were concentrated along the bank of the river, with numerous pillboxes, barbed wire and minefields. Other pillboxes covered the approaches from the south and west, whilst three Pickett-Hamilton turrets were inserted in the centre of the airfield. The airfield's first Battle Headquarters was located in the south-west corner of the airfield, but was replaced with a new one on the north-west side of the airfield.

During the Battle of Britain, the airfield served as an emergency landing ground and then hosted the Fighter Interception Unit until early 1941. The airfield was then extended, a new perimeter road and hardstandings were added and four Over Blister Hangars were erected. In May 1941 an Air-Sea Rescue flight of Lysanders was established at Shoreham, later becoming part of No. 277 Squadron with the addition of two Walruses. During the Dieppe Raid, two squadrons of Hurricanes were based at Shoreham, but returned to their home base afterwards. In April 1943 No. 7 AA Practice Camp was formed at Shoreham to train RAF Regiment gunners, with the Lysanders of No. 1631 Flight providing target-towing facilities. The RAF Regiment camp was located on the north-west side of the airfield and amongst the facilities built was a Gunnery Training Dome.

Later in 1943, No. 345 (Free French) Squadron with Spitfires arrived and was based at the airfield until after D-Day. In September 1944 the airfield was reduced to Care and Maintenance and there was little activity until it was transferred to the Ministry of Civil Aviation in March 1946, to be re-opened in June that year. The airfield finally received a hard runway in 1982 and is today a thriving small airport.

The sites today

Although many of the military airfield buildings at Shoreham have been removed by recent development, there are a few survivors that together form the most complete group of airfield buildings and defences that survive in Sussex. The most important of these is the airport Terminal Building (TQ 2047 0515); completed in 1935 this art-deco building is now a Grade 2 listed building and continues to function as the airport's terminal building with its integral control tower. Adjacent to the Terminal Building is the double hangar originally built in 1934-5 (TQ 2042 0509). It was damaged during an air-raid in the Second World War and reduced to its frame, into which a Blister Hangar was then inserted. Although the original hangar was repaired after the war, and is currently still used, it is planned to replace it in the near future. All of the remaining wartime buildings around the Terminal Building have now been removed. In the south-east corner of the airfield there are two surviving air-raid shelters; the first is adjacent to a car park and is very overgrown (TQ 2079 0528), whilst the second is partly sunken and adjacent to the river embankment (TQ 2073 0537). It is a rectangular brick structure with a concrete roof, having an entrance towards each end protected by an external brick blast wall. All the other air-raid shelters around the airfield have also now been removed.

At the north-east corner of the airfield is the northern Guardroom (TQ 2037 0598), although this is no longer used and is boarded up. Note the change in brickwork; this is the result of rebuilding after it had been struck by a crashing USAAF bomber in 1944. On the north side of the airfield there is a surviving Blister Hangar, although modified and added to in the 1950/60s (TQ 2004 0594); a second Blister Hanger nearby (TQ 1995 0588) has been removed. The unique Gunnery Training Dome is still extant at TQ 1987 0584 (*colour plate 24*). It has suffered from some fire damage and graffiti, but has been repainted and is in a reasonable condition, although requiring some attention. It was associated with the RAF Regiment training camp situated at TQ 1965 0570, although there is no surviving evidence of this camp today.

An overgrown variant pillbox or guard post that covered the approach road to the airfield from the south is located at TQ 2034 0482. It is brick built with a concrete roof and has entrances on its south and west sides protected by external blast walls and a large window/embrasure facing east. The flint wall to its south appears to have been loopholed. The southern Guardroom was located close to the railway underpass and has recently been demolished. The pillboxes on the west side of the airfield (one of which is marked as an OP on the Airfield Plan (TQ 1981 0572)) all appear to have been removed.

The pillboxes and emplacements along the River Adur on the east side of the airfield survive reasonably intact and form a unique group of sites (*72*). The first pillbox is an octagonal-shaped brick structure (*colour plate 25*) with a concrete roof, that has been built into the west slope of the river embankment (TQ 2076 0535). It has steps down to its entrance on the south side protected by a blast wall and inside there are six small embrasures; three of these face across the river and three face across the airfield (*72a*). A second entrance in the north wall provides access into a square open-topped brick annex, which has a concrete base and would have mounted an anti-aircraft machine gun. The next pillbox is situated on the airfield side of the river embankment and is partly sunk into the ground (TQ 2071 0540). It is six-sided, with three small walls each with a small embrasure, facing across the airfield (*72b*). The

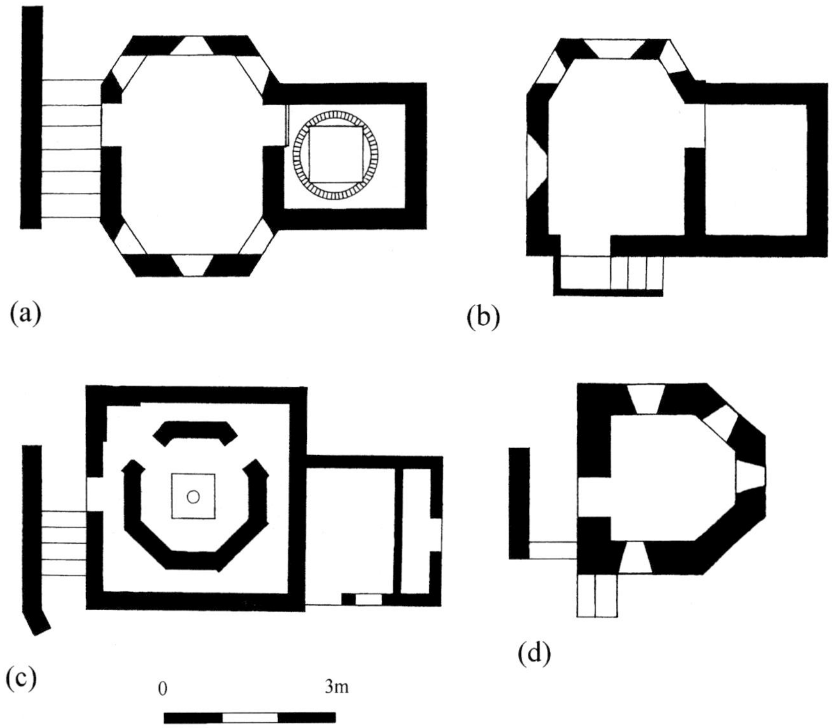

72 Shoreham Airfield Pillboxes: (a) Pillbox with anti-aircraft gun annex (TQ 2076 0535), (b) Pillbox with anti-aircraft machine gun annex (TQ 2071 0540), (c) Type 27 variant pillbox (TQ 2069 0548), (d) Pillbox (TQ 2050 0591). *Adapted from original drawings by Ron Martin*

entrance is on the east side and there may be a further embrasure in the south wall. An entrance in the north wall provides access to an open-topped square anti-aircraft machine gun annex. The interior is flooded, but there appears to be an internal wooden dividing wall in situ. Nearby is a circular raised area, which may have been the position for a Bofors anti-aircraft gun (TQ 2070 0538).

An anti-aircraft gun emplacement, similar to a Type 27 pillbox, is built into the west side of the river embankment at TQ 2069 0548 (*72c*). It has steps, protected by a blast wall, up to the entrance into an open-topped square brick-built emplacement, within which there is an octagonal brick wall enclosing a plinth for mounting an anti-aircraft gun (*73*). A crew and ammunition shelter has been added onto the south side of the emplacement, with an entrance into the larger crew compartment on the west side and an entrance to the ammunition store on the south side; an internal wall divides the two parts. A little further north there is the base of a pillbox that was demolished recently, as it is on the approach path to the airfield runway (TQ 2061 0568). It is built into the river embankment and has steps down and a blast wall on the north side. A circular plinth in the centre of its concrete base may suggest that it was an anti-aircraft emplacement, rather than a pillbox.

73 An anti-aircraft gun emplacement (Type 27 variant) built into the river embankment at Shoreham Airfield (TQ 2069 0548)

The next pillbox is positioned on the river embankment (TQ 2050 0591) and has steps down to the entrance on its north side, protected by a brick blast wall (*72d*). The pillbox is brick-shuttered concrete and has six sides with an embrasure in each of the longer walls on its east and west sides, and embrasures facing south and south-east in two of the three short walls at the south end (*74*). There is a small embrasure facing north above the entrance. The final pillbox is at the north entrance to the airfield, close to the northern Guardhouse, and is constructed from brick-shuttered concrete (TQ 2043 0596). It is similar in design to the previous example, although with thinner walls. It has an entrance on its south side protected by a brick blast wall and four embrasures facing east, north, north-west and west, all of which are bricked-up.

Situated on slightly higher ground in the north-east corner of the airfield is a standard concrete gun emplacement, covering Old Shoreham Bridge (TQ 2046 0592). Located some 15m to its rear is a small brick structure that may have been part of the machine gun firing range that was located here. The Airfield Plan also shows a machine gun post at this location.

The Airfield Plan shows the location of the three Pickett-Hamilton turrets. One of these is currently within the helicopter training area (approx. TQ204057), but is believed to still be extant. The second is in the north-west part of the airfield (approx. TQ200055) adjacent to the current runway and its status is unknown. However, the third is located just in front of the Terminal Building (TQ 2036 0525) and although flooded, its hatch can be lifted to reveal all of the internal fittings still intact (*75*). The Battle Headquarters on the northern side of the airfield was removed when the A27 was widened.

74 This pillbox is positioned on the river embankment on the east side of Shoreham Airfield (TQ 2050 0591)

75 A Pickett-Hamilton turret in front of the terminal building at Shoreham Airfield (TQ 2036 0525). Although fixed in the down position and flooded, the hatch can be opened to reveal all of the internal fittings still in-situ

Directions and access

Shoreham Airport can be reached from the A27 junction to the west of the Shoreham flyover. Follow the signs to the Airport Terminal around the perimeter road, where there is a car park. There is an Archive and Visitor Centre located in the hangar annex beside the Terminal Building and guided tours can be arranged, although it is necessary to book these in advance.

Return to the perimeter road and park in one of the grass car park/viewing areas, from where the air-raid shelters, pillboxes and other emplacements on the east side of the airfield can be visited. To access the footpath that runs along the top of the river embankment, walk to the south-east corner of the airfield, near the railway bridge, where there is a path and bridge onto the footpath. Follow the footpath north, which allows you to gain access to most of the sites, until you reach the road at Old Shoreham Bridge. From here turn south past the northern Guardroom and gun emplacement and return to the car park visiting the remaining sites on the west side of the river embankment.

There is no access to the Gunnery Training Dome or Blister Hangar on the north side of the airfield, or to the Pickett-Hamilton turret, which are all within the airfield perimeter. However, it may be possible to arrange a specific tour of these sites through the Archive and Visitor Centre.

Opening times

Access is possible to the Airport car parks and Terminal Building at any reasonable time. The Archive and Visitor Centre is normally open seven days a week, 10am to 5pm. Tel: 01273 441061, saha@visitorcentre.info

References/Background reading

Ashworth, R.C.B. 1985, *Action Stations 9. Military airfields of the Central South and South-East*, Wellingborough, Patrick Stephens Ltd

Brooks, R.J. 1993, *Sussex Airfields in the Second World War*, Countryside Books, Newbury

Delve, K. 2005, *The Military Airfields of Britain: Southern England*, Marlborough, Crowood Press Ltd

Martin, R.G. 1998-2001, *Shoreham Airfield Pillboxes*, unpublished drawings

Martin, R.G. 2001, *Shoreham Airfield Air Raid Shelters*, unpublished drawings

Roberts, P. 2006, *Shoreham Airport: A Brief History*, The Shoreham Airport Historical Association

Shoreham Airfield Plan No 141, 7372/54 dated 12/10/50 (RAF Museum)

Shoreham Airport Archive and Visitor Centre: www.visitorcentre.info

SITE 38: COOLHAM

Period: **Second World War**

Type of Site: **Advanced landing Ground**

History

The Coolham ALG was built during 1943 in the lead-up to D-Day. Two temporary runways were laid out, broadly orientated north-south and east-west, together with a metalled perimeter track and 36 aircraft dispersal standings. The Technical Site and Communal Site were adjacent to one another off Saucelands Road (TQ121217), which was closed as one of the runways extended across it, whilst the four Blister Hangars were located in the north-west part of the site. The living conditions were described as primitive, with the personnel living in tents and local houses.

In April 1944 the first flying squadrons arrived, comprising three squadrons of No. 133 Airfield, equipped with Mustang fighters. In the run-up to D-Day and immediately afterwards, the squadrons operated deep penetration operations and escort missions. These were replaced in late June by No. 135 Wing operating Spitfire IXs who undertook fighter/bomber missions over Normandy, but then vacated the airfield by the 4 July. The ALG was then left deserted and by the end of the year the temporary runways had been removed.

The site today

Although the site quickly reverted back to agriculture after the war, some parts of the airfield remain to be seen today. Most of the metalled perimeter track can still be seen, with a good section running from TQ 1193 2258 to TQ 1308 2220. At TQ 1188 2191 there is a brick building that was the pump house (*76*) associated with a bulk petrol installation that was located alongside the B2193 road. A Nissen hut can be seen at approximately TQ 1223 2165, at the location of the ration store in the communal site.

76 The Pump House at Coolham ALG

Outside the Selsey Arms in Coolham village is a memorial to the pilots who lost their lives whilst based at Coolham ALG.

Directions and access

The ALG (TQ125224) is signposted for pedestrians off the B2193 south of Coolham village and a footpath follows the line of the original main north-west/south-east orientated runway. It is best to park in the village and walk, as there is nowhere to park on this busy road. The pump house is on private land and can be viewed at a distance from the road, whilst the Nissen hut can be seen from Saucelands Road. Access is only possible by following the sign-posted footpaths.

References/Background reading

Brooks, R.J. 1993, *Sussex Airfields in the Second World War*, Countryside Books, Newbury

Delve, K. 2005, *The Military Airfields of Britain: Southern England*, Marlborough, Crowood Press Ltd

Coolham Layout Plan 609/44 dated Nov 1943 (RAF Museum)

SITE 39: GATWICK

Period: **Second World War**
Type of Site: **Airfield**

History

Gatwick was licensed as an airfield in the 1930s and by 1936 had expanded to include a terminal building, hangars and other developments. In 1937 No. 19 Elementary and Reserve Flying Training School began flying Tiger Moths from Gatwick, and continued to operate a number of different aircraft types until the outbreak of war. During 1940 Gatwick was used by a number of Spitfire squadrons of No. 70 Wing, until these were replaced by the Lysanders of No. 71 Group of Army Cooperation Command. Plagued by waterlogging, two army Track runways were laid in 1941 and at some point six Blister hangars were erected, adding to the existing Bellman Hangar. The terminal building was used as the squadron offices and operations office, with personnel being accommodated in the adjacent racecourse grandstand or in tented camps. Officers were accommodated in various houses around the airfield and had their mess in the Chequers Hotel. Four Bofors 40mm anti-aircraft guns were protecting Gatwick in September 1940.

The airfield was used by Army Cooperation and photographic reconnaissance squadrons equipped with Mustangs and Spitfires from 1941 until after D-Day, when it ceased to be used as an operational base. Gatwick was released from RAF service in 1946 and handed over to the Ministry of Civil Aviation; in 1956 it was selected as the site for London's second airport.

Hammerwood was established in 1943 as one of a number of AOPs bases to prepare AOP squadrons for the forthcoming, it comprised two grass landing strips surrounded by woodland and had its HQ in Hammerwood House (TQ438392). The last squadron to use the base left for France on 14 June 1944; it reverted back to its original owners shortly afterwards.

The site today

A huge amount of development has taken place at Gatwick since 1956, which has removed almost all evidence of the early airfield and its facilities (TQ270404). The only survivor is the original circular terminal building known as 'The Beehive'; this was built in 1936 and is now a listed building (TQ287399). It was connected to the original (now demolished) railway station by an underground walkway.

A number of anti-aircraft towers were located around Gatwick during the Second World War, the last of which was demolished without permission in the late 1990s. This tower was located at Forge Farm, Steers Lane, Crawley (TQ 2911 3943) and was a three-story brick structure within a reinforced concrete frame. The lower storeys contained a stairway to the roof, together with storerooms and accommodation. The roof had two platforms, the larger mounting a Bofors anti-aircraft gun, whilst the smaller platform may have mounted a rangefinder or machine guns. There is no surviving trace of the AOP base at Hammerwood.

Directions and access

'The Beehive' terminal building can be found by taking Beehive Ring Road off the Gatwick Road from the roundabout on the A23.

References/Background reading

Ashworth, R.C.B. 1985, *Action Stations 9. Military airfields of the Central South and South-East*, Wellingborough, Patrick Stephens Ltd

Brooks, R.J. 1993, *Sussex Airfields in the Second World War*, Newbury Countryside Books

Delve, K. 2005, *The Military Airfields of Britain: Southern England*, Marlborough, Crowood Press Ltd

Martin, R.G. 1998, *Anti-aircraft Tower at Forge Farm, Steers Lane, Crawley*, unpublished report and drawing

www.gatwickaviationsociety.org.uk/history.asp

www.subbrit.org.uk/sb-sites/sites/g/gatwick_airport_passenger_subway/index2.shtml

GLOSSARY

AOP	Air Observation Post
BL	Breech Loading
Caponier	Structure connected to a fortress and placed so that weapons from its embrasures can fire along the fortress ditch
Casemate	Protected structure containing a gun position or used as barracks
CP	Command Post
ECB	Emergency Coastal Battery
Embrasure	Small window or opening in defensive work from which weapons can be fired
En-barbette	Raised gun position on a parapet
Flame fougasse	Remote-controlled explosive flame device
GCI	Ground Controlled Interception
Glacis	Cleared area of sloping ground in front of a fortification
HAA	Heavy Anti-Aircraft
LAA	Light Anti-Aircraft
Lunette	Large detached work with flanks and an open ditch
MMG	Medium Machine Gun
MT	Motor Transport
MU	Maintenance Unit
OP	Observation Post
QF	Quick Firing
QL	Decoy Lighting Site
RAF	Royal Air Force
RE	Royal Engineers
RFC	Royal Flying Corps
RM	Rifled Muzzle Loader
RNAS	Royal Naval Air Service
RNR	Royal Navy Reserve
RNVR	Royal Naval Volunteer Reserve
ROC	Royal Observer Corps
SAR	Search and Rescue
SF	Starfish (Special Fires) decoy site
USAAF	United States Army Air Force
USAAS	United States Army Air Service

BIBLIOGRAPHY

Adams, C., Hayes, M., McCann, T.J. & Readman, A. 1995, *West Sussex at War 1939-1945, Local History Mini Guide No. 2*, West Sussex County Council

Angell, S. 1996, *The Secret Sussex Resistance*, Midhurst, Middleton Press

Ashworth, R.C.B. 1985, *Action Stations 9. Military airfields of the Central South and South-East*, Wellingborough, Patrick Stephens Ltd

Bilton, D. 2004, *The Home Front in the Great War*, Barnsley, Pen & Sword Books Limited

Brooks, R.J. 1993 *Sussex Airfields in the Second World War*, Newbury, Countryside Books.

Buchan Innes, G. 2000, *British Airfield Buildings Vol. 2: The Expansion & Inter-War Periods*, Leicester, Midland Publishing

Buckton, H. 1993, *Forewarned is Forearmed*, Leatherhead, Ashford, Buchan & Enright.

Bull, S. 2002, *World War I Trench Warfare (1) 1914-16*, Oxford, Osprey Publishing Ltd

Burgess, P. & Saunders, A. 1990, *Battle over Sussex 1940*, Midhurst, Middleton Press

Burgess, P. & Saunders, A. 1994, *Blitz over Sussex 1941-42*, Midhurst, Middleton Press

Burgess, P. & Saunders, A. 1995, *Bombers over Sussex 1943-45*, Midhurst, Middleton Press

Butler, C. 2007, *East Sussex Under Attack*, Stroud, Tempus Publishing Ltd

Chamberlain, P. & Gander, T. 1975, *Anti-Aircraft Guns*, World War 2 Fact Files, London, Macdonald & Jane's

Clarke, D. 2005, *British Artillery 1914-19: Heavy Artillery*, Oxford, Osprey Publishing Ltd

Cocroft, W.D. & Thomas, R.J.C. 2003, *Cold War: Building for Nuclear Confrontation 1946-1989*, (edited by P.S. Barnwell), Swindon, English Heritage

Crook, P. 1998, *Sussex Home Guard*, Midhurst, Middleton Press

Delve, K. 2005, *The Military Airfields of Britain: Southern England*, Marlborough, Crowood Press Ltd

Dobinson, C. 2000, *Fields of Deception*, London, Methuen Publishing Ltd

Dobinson, C. 2001, *AA Command*, London, Methuen Publishing Ltd

Duffy, C. 1975, *Fire & Stone*, London, David & Charles Ltd

Ellis, C. & Chamberlain, P. (eds) 1975, *Handbook on the British Army 1943*, London, Purnell Book Services Ltd

Evans, M.M. 2004, *Invasion! Operation Sealion 1940*, Harlow, Pearson Education Ltd

Fleming, P. 1957, *Invasion 1940*, London, Rupert Hart-Davis

Foot, W. 2006, *Beaches, fields, streets and hills: the anti-invasion landscapes of England*, CBA Research Report 144, York, Council for British Archaeology

Foot, W. 2006, *The Battlefields That Nearly Were*, Stroud, Tempus Publishing Ltd

Forty, G. 2000, *British Army Handbook 1939-1945*, London, Chancellor Press

Goodwin, J.E. 1985, *The Military Defence of West Sussex*, Midhurst, Middleton Press

Goodwin, J.E. 1994, *Fortification of the South Coast: The Pevensey, Eastbourne and Newhaven Defences 1750-1945*, Worthing, JJ Publications

Goodwin, J.E. 2000, *Military Signals from the South Coast*, Midhurst, Middleton Press

Grehan, J. 2001, *Battles & Battlefields of Sussex*, Storrington, Historic Military Press

Greig, I., Leslie, K., Readman, A. 1994, *D-Day West Sussex*, WSCC, Chichester

Grieves, K. 2004, *Sussex in the First World War*, Sussex Record Society Volume 84

Harrington, P. 2004, *English Civil War Archaeology*, London, English Heritage/B.T. Batsford
Haythornthwaite, P. 1996, *The English Civil War 1642-1651*, London, Arms & Armour Press
Haythornthwaite, P. 1998, *The Armies of Wellington*, London, Brockhampton Press
Hayward, J. 2001, *The Bodies on the Beach*, Dereham, CD41 Publishing
Henry, C. 2003, *British Napoleonic Artillery 1793-1815 (2) Siege and Coastal Artillery*, Oxford, Osprey Publishing Ltd
Hewitt, P. 2004, *Chichester Remembered*, Chichester, Phillimore & Co Ltd
Hudson, A. 1984, 'Volunteer Soldiers in Sussex during the Revolutionary and Napoleonic Wars, 1793-1815', *Sussex Archaeological Collections* 122, 165-181
Hudson, A. 1986, 'Napoleonic Barracks in Sussex', *Sussex Archaeological Collections* 124, 267-268
Hylton, S. 2004, *Kent and Sussex 1940*, Barnsley, Pen & Sword Books Ltd
Kitchen, F. 1986, 'The Ghastly War-Flame: Fire Beacons in Sussex until the mid seventeenth century', *Sussex Archaeological Collections* 124, 179-91
Leppard, M.J. 2001, *A History of East Grinstead*, Chichester, Phillimore & Co Ltd
Leslie, K. & Short, B. (eds) 1999, *An Historical Atlas of Sussex*, Chichester, Phillimore
Longmate, N. 2001, *Island Fortress: The Defence of Great Britain 1603-1945*, London, Pimlico
Longstaff-Tyrell, P. 1999, *Tyrrell's List*, Polegate, Gote House Publishing
Longstaff-Tyrrell, P. 2000, *Front-Line Sussex*, Stroud, Sutton Publishing Ltd
Longstaff-Tyrrell, P. 2002, *Barracks to Bunkers*, Stroud, Sutton Publishing Ltd
Lower, M.A. (ed.) 1870, *A Survey of the Coast of Sussex made in 1587*, Lewes, W.E. Barber
Lowry, B. (ed.) 1996, *20th Century Defences in Britain: An Introductory Guide*, York, Council for British Archaeology
Lowry, B. 1998, 'Hunting the Survivors of Dad's Army', *British Archaeology No* 40
Lowry, B. 2004, *British Home Defences 1940-45*, Oxford, Osprey Publishing Ltd
Lowry, B. 2006, *Discovering Fortifications: from the Tudors to the Cold War*, Princes Risborough, Shire Publications Ltd
McCutcheon, C. 2006, *Home Guard Manual 1941*, Stroud, Tempus Publishing Ltd
Mace, M.F. 1996, *Frontline Sussex: The Defence Lines of West Sussex 1939-1945*, Storrington, Historic Military Press
Mace, M.F. 1997, *Sussex Wartime Relics and Memorials*, Storrington, Historic Military Press
Marsden, P. 1987, *The Historic Wrecks of South-East England*, Norwich, Jarrold & Sons Ltd
Osborne, M. 2004, *Defending Britain*, Stroud, Tempus Publishing Ltd
Planel, P. 1995, *A Teacher's Guide to Battlefields Defence Conflict and Warfare*, London, English Heritage
Price, A. 1990, *The Hardest Day*, London, Arrow Books
Rowland, D. 2001, *Coastal Blitz*, Seaford, S.B. Publications
Sanders, I.J. 2005, *Pillboxes: Images of an Unfought Battle*, Lightning Source UK Ltd
Saunders, A. 1997, *Channel Defences*, London, English Heritage/B.T. Batsford
Shores, C. 1991, *Fledgling Eagles*, London, Grub Street
Short, J. 2005, *The Remains of a Military Landscape*, unpublished MA thesis, University of Leicester
Williamson, J.A. 1959, *The English Channel*, London, Collins
Wills, H. 1985, *Pillboxes: A study of U.K. Defences 1940*, London, Leo Cooper
W.S.C.C. 1977, *Archaeology in West Sussex – A Field Guide*, Chichester, West Sussex county Council

INDEX

Entries in italics refer to illustrations